When you buy an authentic shoe made by Nike or Adidas, you reward the designers, the athletes, and the factory workers for their hard work. You also reward the brands for delivering quality materials, researched ergonomic function, and ethical labor practices.

When you mistakenly buy a counterfeit shoe, you are supporting a criminal enterprise. The bandit factories making counterfeit shoes have no reason to test materials, fit, or quality. These unauthorized factories and the criminal middlemen that buy and import the shoes are only interested in making money and will deliver substandard or even dangerous merchandise. They prey on consumers and brands, stealing money and delivering inferior products.

You can put these criminals out of business and protect yourself by learning how to spot fake sneakers.

SHOEMAKERS ACADEMY

Online Shoemaking Courses for all levels of Shoemakers, Shoe Designers, Developers, and Brand builders.

Expand your skills and knowledge in modern shoe design, manufacturing sourcing, and footwear brand development.

Jumpstart your career. Launch your shoe brand.

Available worldwide, On-demand, Online, and on your schedule. Start Today!

Textbooks Available now:
How Shoes are Made
Footwear Pattern Making and Last Design
Shoe Material Design Guide
How to Start Your Own Shoe Company
How to Spot Fake Sneakers
Cómo se hacen los zapatos
Cómo empezar tu propia empresa de calzado
Guía para el diseño de materiales de calzado
Patronaje de calzado y diseño de hormas
鞋子是怎样制成的

HOW TO SPOT FAKE SNEAKERS

Written and Edited by
Wade, Alex, Erik, and Andrea Motawi

ISBN-13: 978-1-7358833-3-5
ISBN-10: 1-7358833-3-6
USA Copyright © 2020

Online Shoemaking Courses
Shoemaking for Designers and Brand Builders
How to Select Shoe Materials
Sneaker Authentication Basics
Creating Footwear Specifications
Footwear Cost Calculation
Footwear Cost Engineering
Footwear Inspection and Quality Control
Building a Modern Shoe Factory
Footwear Sustainability Strategies
Footwear Fitting & Comfort
Footwear Import Duty
Starting Your Shoe Business
Shoe Types and Constructions
How to Design Shoes
DIY Shoemaking for Beginners
The Footwear Process Development to Production
Footwear Development Factory Communications
Footwear Marketing & Merchandising

Dear Readers,
This book was written to educate, inform, and inspire the next generation of shoe designers, shoe developers, shoemakers, and footwear entrepreneurs. Our goal is to help prepare people for fulfilling careers in the world of shoes.

Enjoy!
Special thanks to:
Andrea, Alex & Erik, Karim, Halla, Mom, Joanne, Dave, Alfredo, Jason, David, Lizzie, Johnson, Steve, Lenny, Bernie, Jenny, Simon, Ben, David,- Jack, Gary, Jean Marc, Suresh, Abdón and Paolo.

Thanks to all my working friends in the USA, China, Hong Kong, Korea, Taiwan, Vietnam and Europe.

HOW TO SPOT FAKE SNEAKERS

How to Inspect and Authenticate Air Jordan, Nike, Adidas, and Vans Sneakers

ALEX, ERIK & WADE MOTAWI

PART 1
HOW TO AUTHENTICATE SNEAKERS

PART 2
SNEAKER PRODUCT KNOWLEDGE

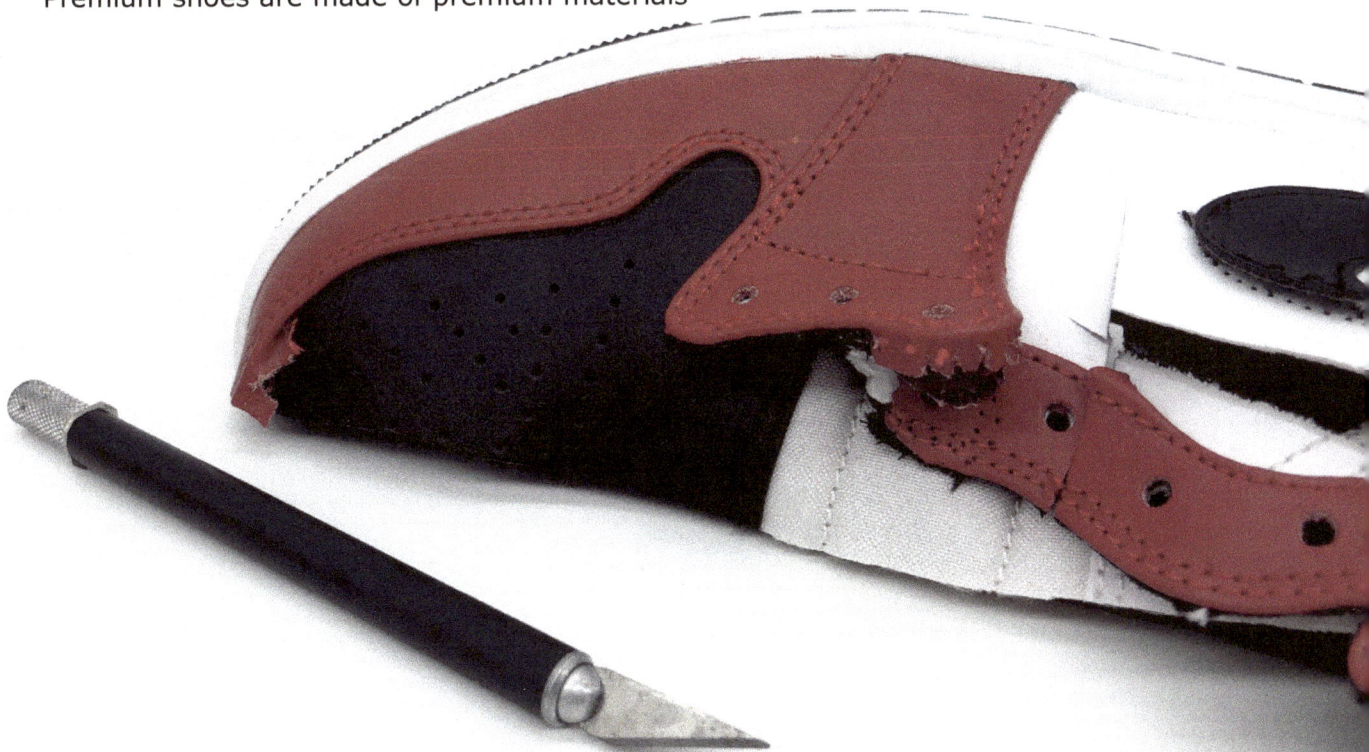

Part 1

Chapter 1 : Sneaker Authentication Basics

How do I spot fake sneakers?

There is no "easy," "works every time, " way to spot a fake shoe. With the goals of misleading consumers and siphoning money away from the brands, counterfeiters have worked for years studying the iconic models of Nike and Adidas. To defeat the counterfeiters, you need to learn how the big brands make shoes and the level of quality they demand from their partner shoe factories. You will start by learning the basics of sneaker construction and fully understanding what quality footwear looks like.

How to Spot Fake Sneakers will be your guide. The team at SneakerFactory.net has been authenticating and inspecting Sneakers for years. We have also been buying fake shoes for analysis in our lab. We share what we have learned to help you avoid the rip-offs and replicas that now plague the sneaker market.

What are the basics of sneaker authentication?

Every counterfeit shoe will have a different tell, flaw, or feature you need to look for when making your authentication. The flaw could be in the packaging, construction, quality, or materials. To find the flaws, you will need to follow a systematic authentication checklist.

Sneaker Authentication Basics:

1.   Product Provenance
    Does this shoe have a reliable provenance?

2.   Footwear Construction
    Is this shoe and its componentry made using the correct construction techniques?

3.   Quality Inspections
    Is this shoe made with the care and quality expected from a big brand?

4.   Sneaker Product Knowledge
    Does this sneaker have the correct design details we know to expect?

Product Provenance

I like to start an authentication by considering the provenance. A solid provenance is a great indication of authenticity, while a missing or incomplete provenance tells you to be on guard for a fake.

Provenance is a record of ownership or origin of a product. For sneakers, provenance can be proven or established in several ways. First, look for a purchase receipt from a reputable source such as a Nike Store, Footlocker, GOAT, or StockX. An original shoe box with scannable bar codes and a matching pair of shoes is another good place to start. Consumers should use caution when buying a new shoe that is missing its box. Also, make sure to gauge the price. If the price looks too good to be true, you are most likely not getting the real deal. Additionally, when buying from a shoe trader, make sure to check every shoe. It is common for shoe traders to have a mix of both real and fake products.

Footwear Construction

Understanding how a shoe is made and why it's made that way is very important when authenticating. To authenticate a shoe, you must understand exactly what you are looking at. You need to know the parts of a shoe, the construction processes, and the materials. To study a shoe, you must speak the language of sneakers. What do you call that thing on the end of a shoelace? What is the name for the part of the shoe on top of your toes? If you don't know what vulcanization is or what board-lasting means, the authentication process will be much harder.

Quality Inspections

A complete understanding of what high-quality shoes look like is critical to sneaker authentication. Once you are familiar with what Adidas or Nike's level of quality looks like, you will be able to spot fake shoes from miles away. Fake shoes all seem to have one thing in common. Their quality is terrible. The goal of the bandit factory is to make the shoes as cheap as possible. Without any quality inspectors from Nike or Adidas checking the details, factories make the shoes quickly, order materials from the cheapest suppliers, and don't waste any time testing the raw materials or the finished shoes.

Sneaker Product Knowledge

Product knowledge is the backbone of sneaker authentication. Knowing what is "correct" is only learned through experience and access to resources. If you are familiar with all the design and construction details of the Nike Air Jordan 1 and know what color materials Nike used, you can spot the fakes. The sneaker market is huge! With so many special colorways and material configurations, it can be a daunting task to know if the shoe is something authentic by Nike. The blue shoe with red accents may be a Footlocker special made for one delivery only in 2018. You may never be able to find a record of that specific version online. High-quality photos from online sites like StockX and GOAT can be incredibly valuable in authentication if you know what to look for.

Chapter 2 : Product Provenance

Provenance
prov·e·nance   / prävənəns/ noun

*"a record of ownership of a work of art or an
antique, used as a guide to authenticity or quality."*

*"The place of origin or earliest known history of something. The beginning of something's existence;
something's origin."*

What is the provenance of a sneaker?
Ultimately, we all want to know if the shoe we have in our hands or that we see on eBay is "real." In this
case, real means: made by an authorized sub-contracting factory. Nike and Adidas do not own factories.
Nike shoes are ALL made by sub-contractors. Is this a bad idea? No. The people at Nike are masters at
sports marketing, shoe design, product development, human sports performance, and promotion. It's okay
to leave the assembly of the bits and pieces to specialists that are more qualified and experienced in that
area.

Nike shoes are made in Asia. Fake Nike's are also made in Asia but at factories that are not staffed with
Nike employees, inspectors, and are not buying materials from Nike-approved suppliers.

Product Provenance Guidelines
1.   Price
2.   Location
3.   Box
4.   Bar Code

Is the price right?

Do you know the correct retail or market price for the shoe? Check online at a reputable website like Nike.com for a new shoe, or StockX.com and GOAT.com for a color or style that is out of production.

Does the price for the shoes seem too low? Why are $145.00 shoes selling for $65.00? Are they used? Are they dirty or damaged in some way? If they are in new condition, why are they so cheap? This is the basic "smell test" for product provenance. If something seems fishy about the price, then walk away.

How can fake shoes be so cheap? Counterfeiters can sell shoes at low prices because they don't manufacture them as quality products, don't have to pay royalties to designers or athletes, and don't pay marketing expenses or business taxes. Additionally, counterfeiters don't provide customer service or deal with product returns.

See here how a counterfeiter selling a copy design online can profit off the back of a shoe brand.

Shoe Factory		Shoe Brand		Shoe Store		Shoe Buyers
	$25.00		$65.00		$150.00	

Shoe Factory		Black Market traders and Counterfeiters			Shoe Buyers
	$15.00		$50.00		

The purchase location

Where is the shoe for sale, and who is selling it? Does the seller have a good reputation? Are they likely to be an authorized seller?

An authorized seller is a store with a buying account directly with Nike, Adidas, or their local representative. Think of the big box sports stores that sell hundreds of shoes; these stores are all authorized. A guy selling shoes at the swap meet off a blanket is surely not authorized. What about a small sports store in China, Poland, Spain, or Turkey? If they have a selection of shoes and clothing, they may be authorized; if they only have a few pieces and not a complete size run, you should be wary.

The shoebox

Are the shoes in their original box? A high-quality shoebox with foil stamping, embossed logos, multi-color ink, and metal pull grommets costs $2.00 or more.

For counterfeiters, cost is critical, and the cost of the shoebox plus the extra space it requires during shipping are significant. Thus, counterfeiters don't often waste time copying the shoe box exactly and often bulk pack the shoes in plastic bags instead. You can authenticate the box by its quality and print details.

A damaged box is not direct evidence of fake shoes, but a missing box is a good reason to be suspicious.

UPC's and Barcodes

Counterfeiters take steps to make the packaging look real and often apply fake UPC and barcodes on the packaging. Every product sold by Nike and Adidas has its own Universal Product Code (UPC) assigned to it according to its size and color. Use your computer or a cellphone application to look up or scan the UPC code and barcode. If you can't confirm the codes match the shoes you have in your hands, be suspicious.

Also, be sure to check the country of origin label on the shoe and the shoebox to make sure it matches.

6

Chapter 3 : Footwear Construction

To authenticate a shoe, you must first understand how shoes are made and know the names of all the shoe parts. A shoe inspection checklist can not help you if you don't know what a topline or Strobel sock is. So, let's discuss the basic parts of a shoe and the most common construction processes used to make classic and modern sneakers.

What is a shoe last?
The last is a roughly foot-shaped form made of molded plastic, carved wood, or cast aluminum. The shape of the last determines the fit, performance, ergonomics, and styling of a shoe. It is also what makes a shoe suitable for playing basketball, climbing mountains, or running a marathon.

The shoe last is the starting point of every sneaker design. The last is the center of the entire shoemaking process. The shoe designer starts with the last and builds the shoe outward. The last is critical to the shape of the shoe. The last sets the size, silhouette, and outline of the shoe.

When a shoe is in production, the stitched pattern will be stretched over the last to create the final shape. This operation is called "lasting." There are several different lasting techniques used to pull the patterns into shape. These include force/Strobel lasting, board lasting, string lasting, toe lasting, heel lasting, hand lasting, and machine lasting. Once the shoe upper is pulled tight to the last, the outsole can be attached. The last holds the soft upper in place while the outsole is attached using glue.

The parts of a sneaker

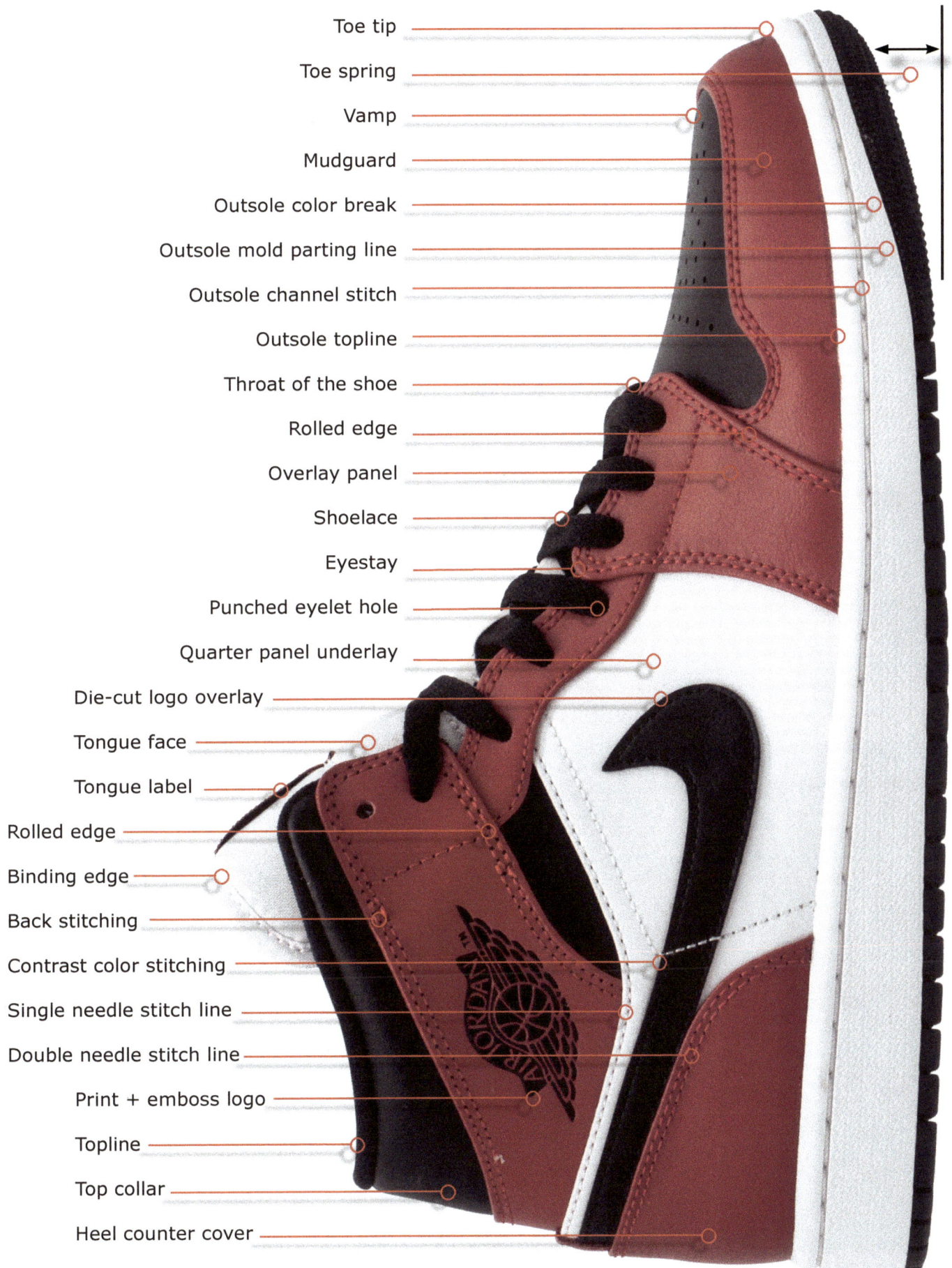

Toe tip

Toe spring

Vamp

Mudguard

Outsole color break

Outsole mold parting line

Outsole channel stitch

Outsole topline

Throat of the shoe

Rolled edge

Overlay panel

Shoelace

Eyestay

Punched eyelet hole

Quarter panel underlay

Die-cut logo overlay

Tongue face

Tongue label

Rolled edge

Binding edge

Back stitching

Contrast color stitching

Single needle stitch line

Double needle stitch line

Print + emboss logo

Topline

Top collar

Heel counter cover

Basic sneaker upper construction: Strobel lasting vs. board lasting

Strobel Lasting

Strobel, slip, force, or California lasting are the most common shoe constructions for casual and athletic sneakers. Once the upper is complete, a "sock" or bottom is added to "close" the bottom of the upper. During the final assembly process, the upper is heated and slipped onto the last; then, it is cooled, causing the material to tighten on the last.

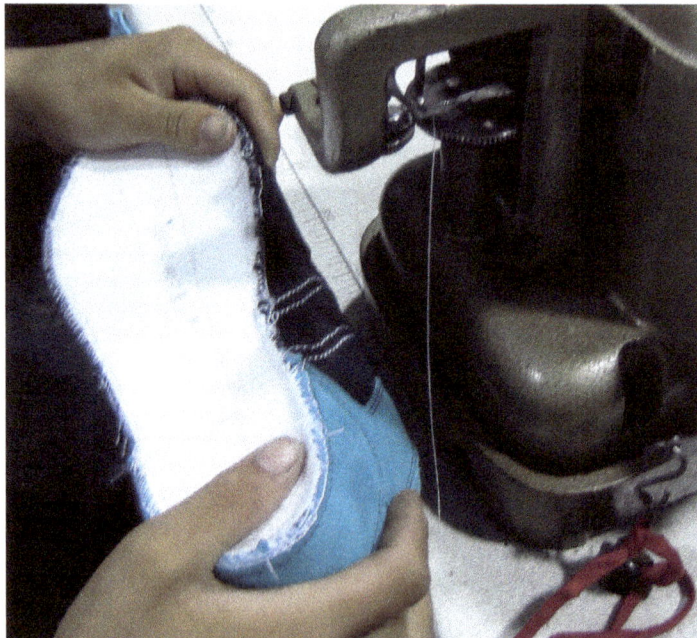

Here the Strobel sock is attached to the upper.

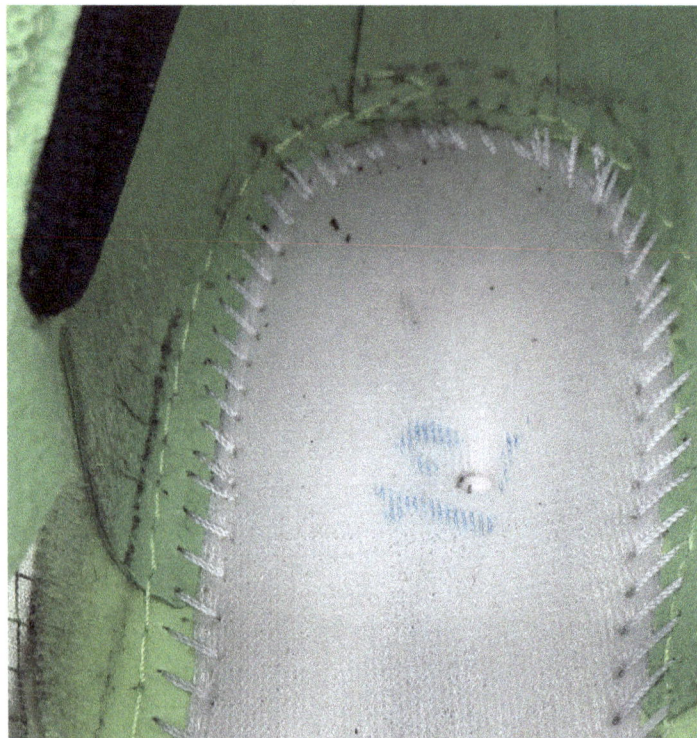

This is what the Strobel sock looks like inside the shoe. You will need to lift the footbed to see the stitching.

Board lasting

Board lasting is a very common process used to make any shoe requiring a stiff bottom. The open upper is placed into a lasting machine that grips the upper and pulls it down onto the last. The last has been prepared with a paperboard or plastic lasting board temporarily attached to the bottom.

In one operation, the lasting machine pulls the upper tight around the last and injects glue between the upper and the lasting board. A heel-lasting machine and some hand pulling will complete the operation before the outsole is attached.

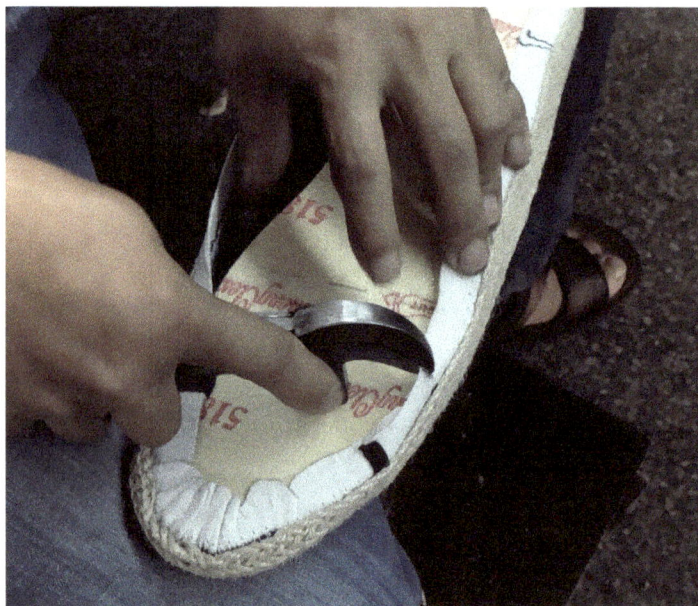

Here a worker is using lasting pliers to wrap the upper over the edge of a lasting board.

This is what a board lasted shoe looks like inside - no edge stitching.

The parts of a sneaker

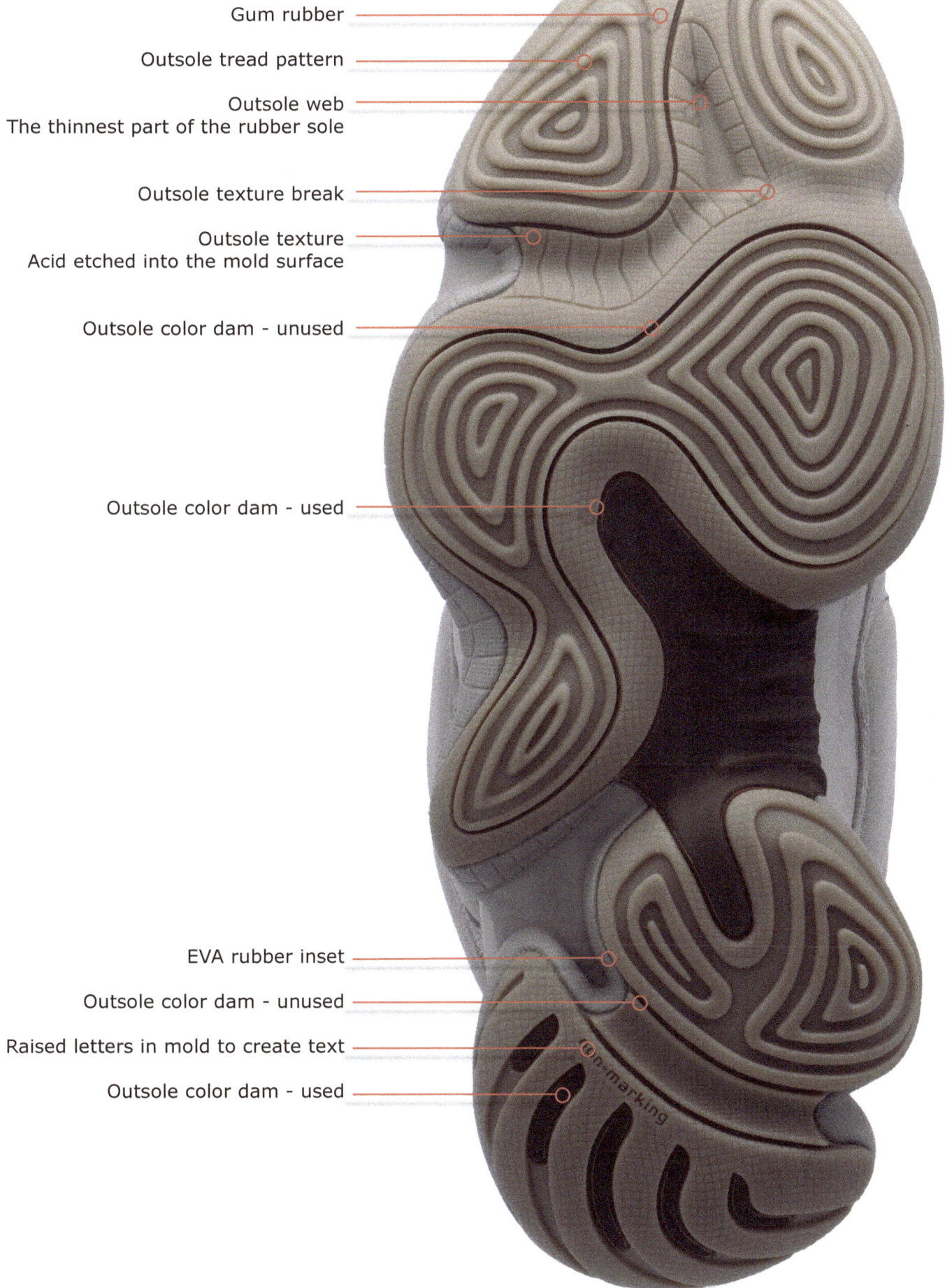

Gum rubber

Outsole tread pattern

Outsole web
The thinnest part of the rubber sole

Outsole texture break

Outsole texture
Acid etched into the mold surface

Outsole color dam - unused

Outsole color dam - used

EVA rubber inset

Outsole color dam - unused

Raised letters in mold to create text

Outsole color dam - used

The parts of a sneaker

Toe tip

Vulcanized foxing tape

Vamp

Vulcanized rubber stripe

Throat of the shoe

Die-cut edge

Eyestay overlay panel

Shoelace

Pinched eyelet hole

Quarter panel underlay

Medial side / Inside of the shoe

Lateral side / Outside of the shoe

Tongue face

Eyestay lining

Tongue binding edge

Turned seam

Collar lining

Footbed / Insole

Heel logo screen print

Collar padding

Top collar

Heel counter lining

11

The inside of a cold cement sneaker

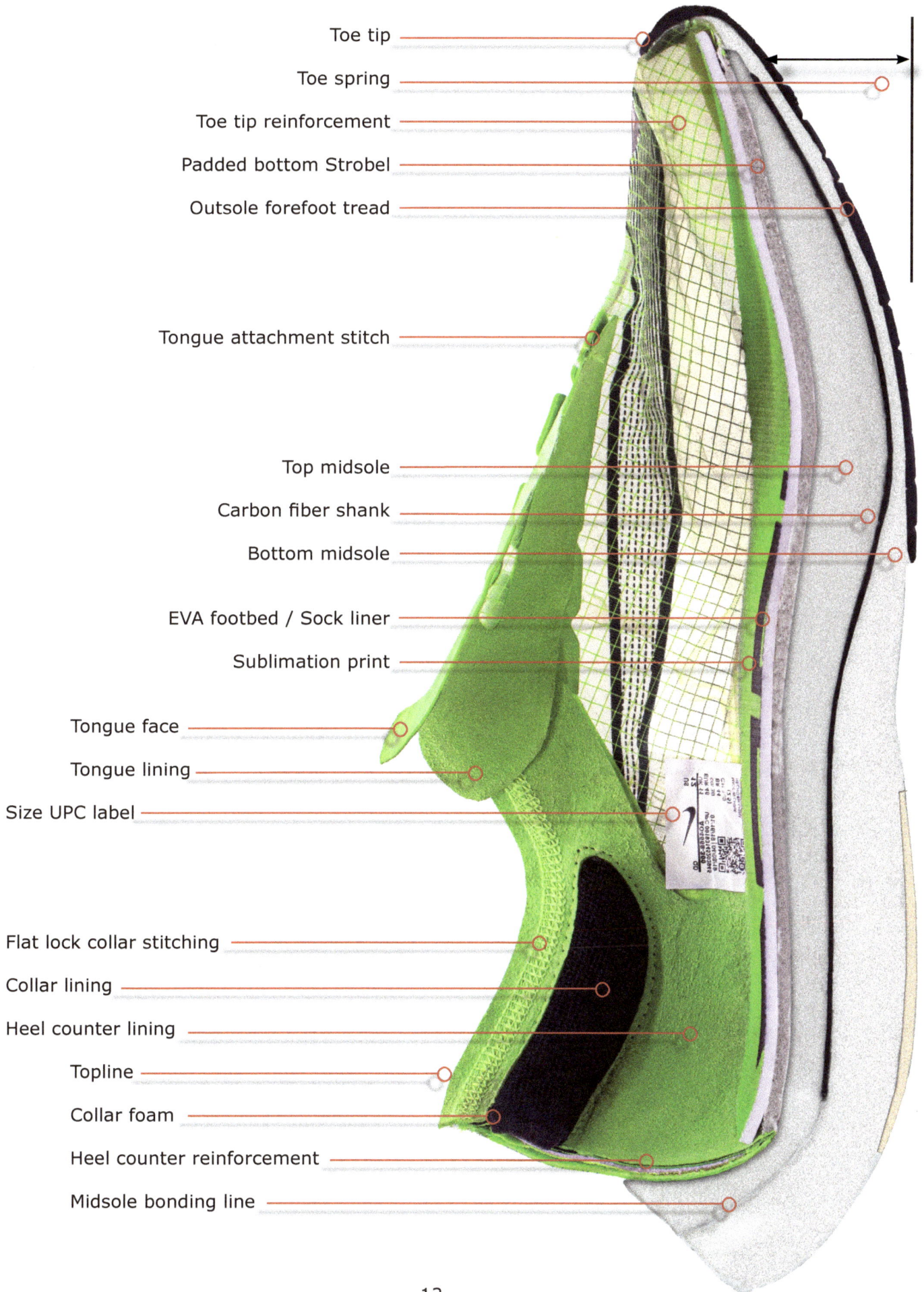

Toe tip

Toe spring

Toe tip reinforcement

Padded bottom Strobel

Outsole forefoot tread

Tongue attachment stitch

Top midsole

Carbon fiber shank

Bottom midsole

EVA footbed / Sock liner

Sublimation print

Tongue face

Tongue lining

Size UPC label

Flat lock collar stitching

Collar lining

Heel counter lining

Topline

Collar foam

Heel counter reinforcement

Midsole bonding line

Footwear construction: Vulcanizing

Let's review how the classics are built. Vans and Converse shoes are made using the vulcanization process. To make the Vans Old Skool shoe, the factory wraps strips of raw rubber around the shoe to make the outsole sidewalls. The entire shoe is then "cooked" to vulcanize the rubber parts.

Here you can see a Vans sneaker board lasted and vulcanized.

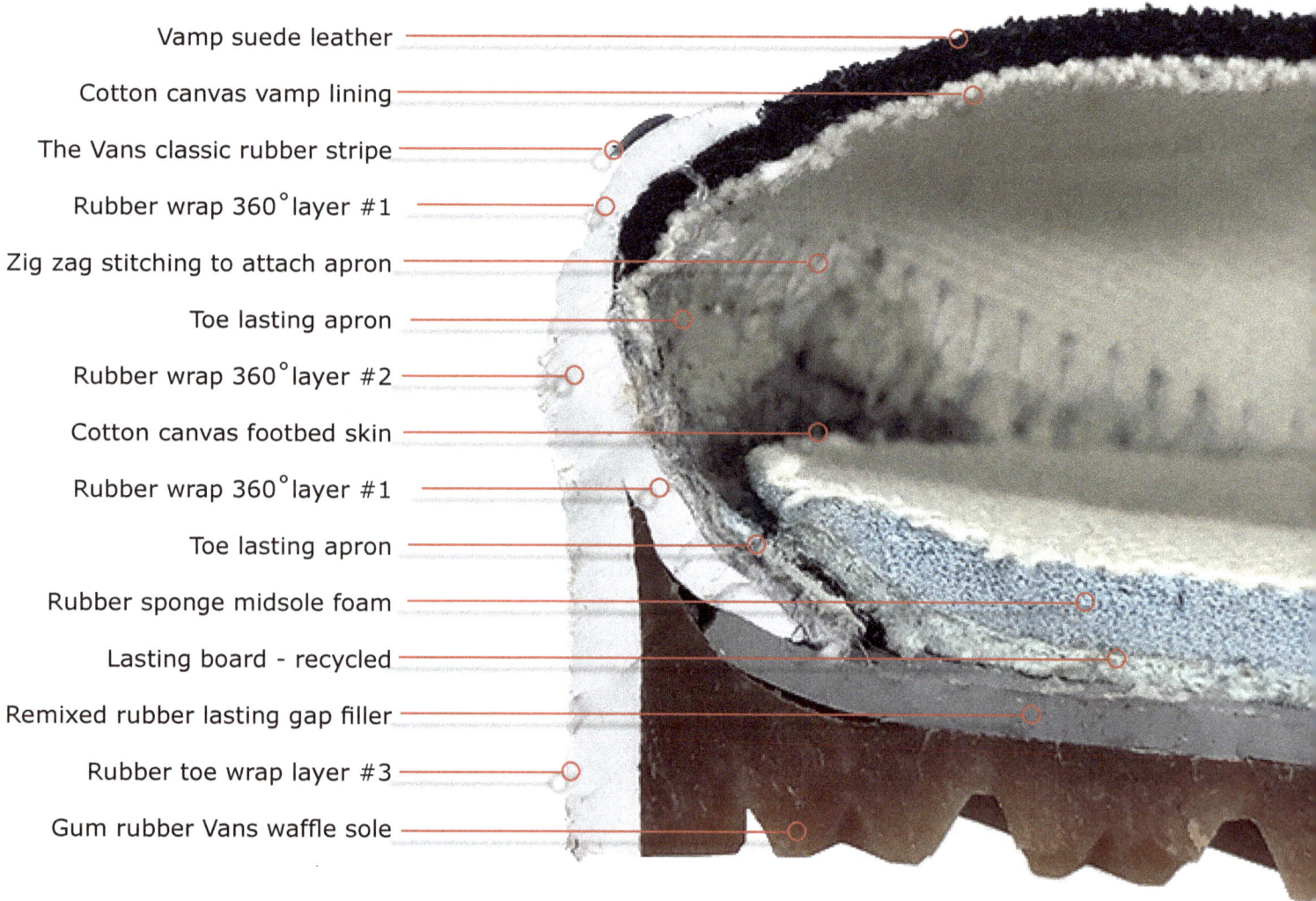

Vamp suede leather

Cotton canvas vamp lining

The Vans classic rubber stripe

Rubber wrap 360° layer #1

Zig zag stitching to attach apron

Toe lasting apron

Rubber wrap 360° layer #2

Cotton canvas footbed skin

Rubber wrap 360° layer #1

Toe lasting apron

Rubber sponge midsole foam

Lasting board - recycled

Remixed rubber lasting gap filler

Rubber toe wrap layer #3

Gum rubber Vans waffle sole

Inside a board lasted shoe

When inspecting a board-lasted shoe, you may find the footbed and lasting board are bonded together and glued down. You may not be able to see what is inside without damaging the shoe.

If you can remove the footbed, you may see some upper stitching around the edge; this stitching will run parallel along the edge. These are not Strobel stitches.

13

Footwear construction: Cold Cement

The more modern way to make a sneaker is called cold cement. "Cold" because the shoe is not cooked and "cement" because the outsole and upper are glued together with contact cement.

Air Jordan 1 is an example of a cold cement shoe made by the Strobel lasting process.

Vamp leather

Toe tip stitching

Skived and wrapped leather edge

Vamp lining foam layer

Toe tip leather

Vamp lining fabric

Rubber cupsole sidewall

Channel stitching line

Mold parting line / color break

Strobel stitch closes upper

Footbed with foam padding

Strobel sock with foam padding

Cup sole rubber outsole tread

Inside a Strobel lasted shoe

When inspecting a Strobel shoe, you should be able to peel up the footbed. In most sneakers, the footbed is held in place with tacky glue and not permanently fixed.

Under the footbed you will see the perpendicular Strobel stitching running the full 360° around the bottom of the shoe. In this shoe, you can see the long loose threads from the channel stitching operations.

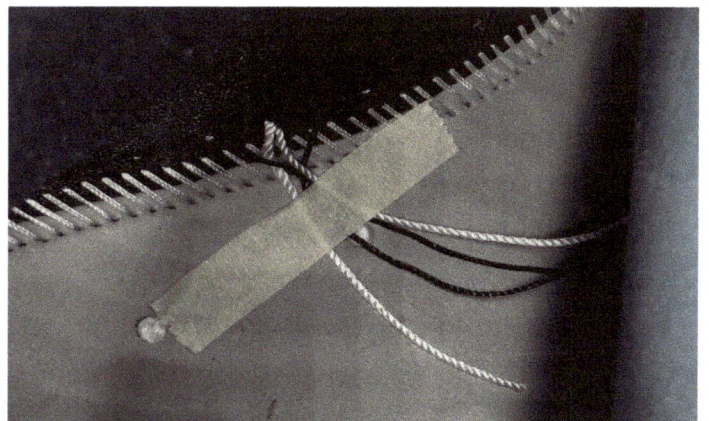

14

SNEAKER CONSTRUCTION TERMS

Action leather
Sueded cow leather that is covered with a thin coating of Polyurethane. The coating may be any color and may be embossed with a roller. The final product is generally a solid color leather looking product. This material is still classified as leather for import duty. Almost all white sneakers are made with action leather.

Aglet
The aglet is that little piece of plastic or metal on the end of the shoelace.

Shoe cement bonding margin
The amount of space required to have a strong cement bond. If the rubber has only a 2mm bonding margin, the outsole may peel off the upper. A 12mm bonding margin would be better.

Chemi-sheet
A non-woven reinforcement material that is impregnated with a chemical hardener that sets with the application of heat or another chemical. Used commonly for heel counter reinforcement on inexpensive shoes.

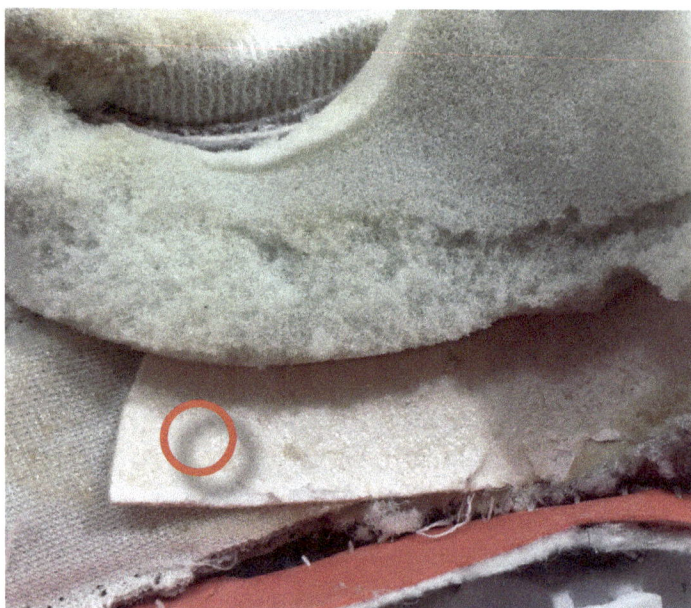

Shoe collar or top line
The opening area of a shoe at the top.

Rubber sole color dam
A color dam on a shoe bottom is a raised ridge and/or groove in a mold to stop the flow of rubber. A sneaker shoe bottom will have color dams dividing all the colors on the sole.

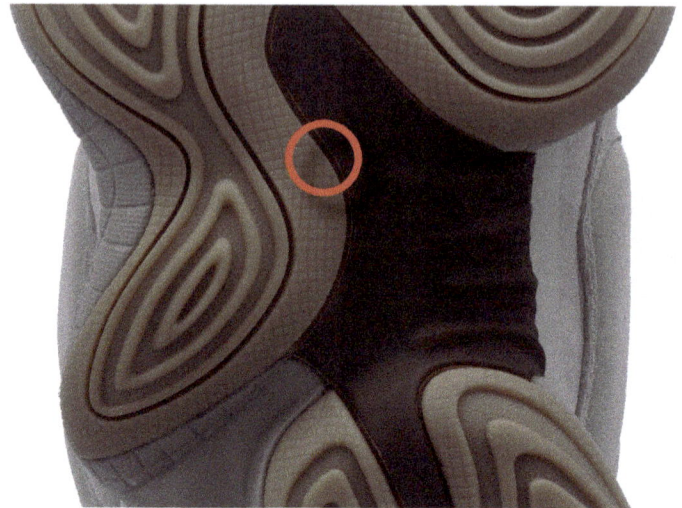

Cupsole or cupsole unit
A shoe outsole unit made of one piece of rubber. Called a cupsole because the sole unit "cups" the upper. Inside the cup can be EVA foam or rubber ribbed egg-crate pattern.

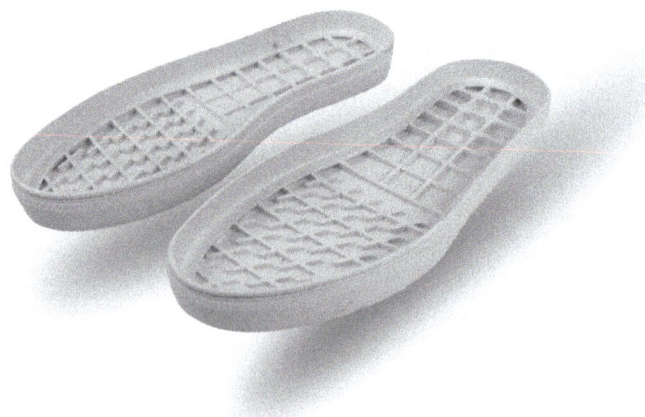

Cut and buff midsole
The cut and buff shoe midsole is the classic running shoe construction. The Nike Cortez and many New Balance classics use this assembly method. A cut and buff midsole is made by cementing a profile cut EVA to a flat rubber midsole. The profile of the EVA makes the toe tip thinner and the heel thicker. Once the EVA is bonded to the rubber, the parts are die-cut to the correct outline shape. The assembly is taken to a grinding stone to have the side angle buffed.

Die-cut EVA midsole
The die-cut EVA midsole is a simple way to add cushioning foam to the bottom of a shoe. The shoe sole will have a cavity molded into the rubber. A piece of die-cut foam is simply glued into the cavity. The die-cut EVA midsole can be flat, or can be profile cut. This EVA is not visible from the outside of the shoe. The sole unit will surround it, and it will be under the lasting board or Strobel sock.

Durometer
Durometer is the hardness of a material. You will need to specify the durometer of all the rubber, foam, and plastic parts. You will need two different durometer testers. Asker "C" is the EVA standard. 25 "C" is very soft, 55 "C" is a standard midsole, and 85 "C" is like wood. For rubber and plastic, you will need a Shore "A" tester. For a rubber outsole Shore "A" 55 is good. Above 60, your rubber will be stiff, heavy, and slippery. The durometer scale was defined by Albert Ferdinand Shore, who developed a measurement device to measure Shore hardness in the 1920s.
Shore 20A = rubber band, Shore 40A = pencil eraser, Shore 60A = car tire tread, Shore 80A = leather belt, Shore 100A = shopping cart wheel

CM EVA or EVA foam
Compression Molded EVA or Ethylene Vinyl Acetate. A foam midsole material that offers good cushioning and compression set. Nike likes to call their EVA "Phylon," it is the same material regardless of the name you call it. EVA is the most common foam for shoe midsoles. Easy to form by cutting, molding, or injecting. It's light and durable. EVA can be made in many grades depending on the compound. More or less filler, more or less vinyl acetate in the mix. EVA foam can be made pillow soft or rock hard.

EVA
Ethylene vinyl acetate is the copolymer of ethylene and vinyl acetate. The weight percent of vinyl acetate varies from 10 to 40%, with the remainder being ethylene. EVA is the most common foam used for shoe cushioning. It can be hot or cold-pressed, made in any color, and in a range of hardnesses.

Eyelet
A hole through which you lace up a shoe.

Eyestay
The part around the lace opening (throat of the shoe). Can feature webbings, eyelets, etc.

Footbed
Footbed, or insole, or sock liner. This is the foam-padded mesh that your foot stands on. It may be removable or cemented in place. In high-end shoes, the footbed will be molded EVA or PU foam. In low-end shoes, it will be die-cut EVA.

Foxing tape
The foxing tape is the rubber band that makes the sidewall of the shoe sole on vulcanized shoes.

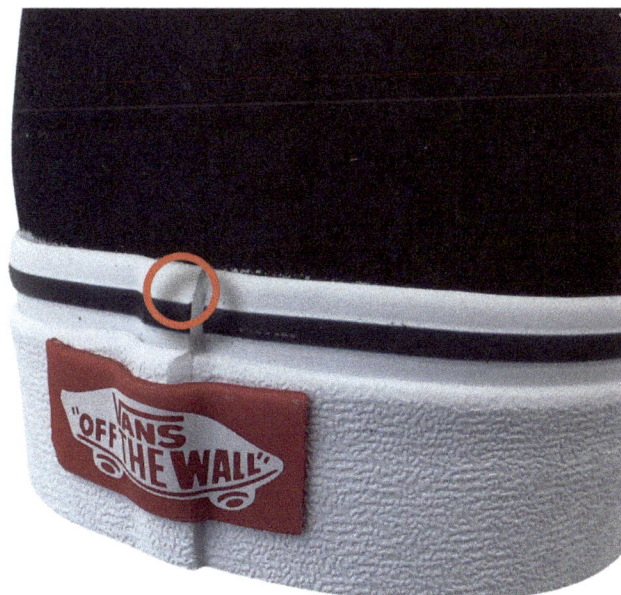

Full grain leather

Full grain leather refers to hides that have not been sanded, buffed, or snuffed (as opposed to top-grain or corrected leather) to remove imperfections (or natural marks) on the hide's surface. The grain remains, allowing the fiber strength and durability. The grain also has breathability, resulting in less moisture from prolonged contact. Rather than wearing out, it will develop a patina over time. High-quality leather furniture and footwear are often made from full-grain leather.

Glue allowance or glue line

The standard glue allowance is 2mm. The outsole glue may be applied up to 2mm above the outsole top edge. This allows for a good bond. Too much glue can turn yellow later.

Heel counter

Internal or external, the heel counter is the pattern part that covers the heel of the shoe. The internal heel counter can be made of rubber (for vulcanized shoes), thermoplastic (for cold cement shoes), chemi-sheet (for inexpensive shoes), or leather (for dress shoes). Depending on the shoe type, the counter can be thin and soft or stiff and sturdy.

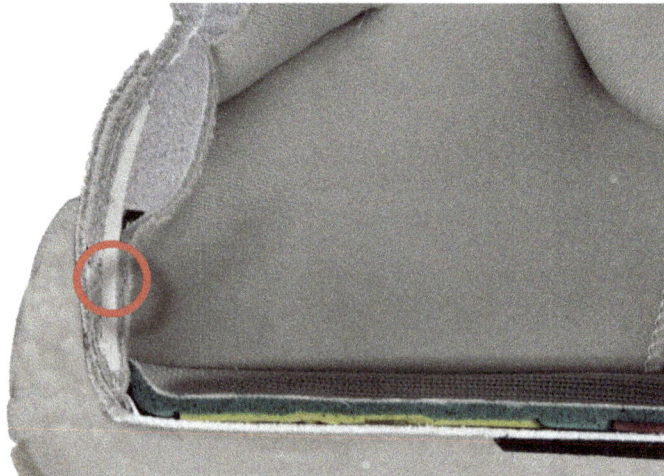

Heel notch

The heel notch is at the back of a shoe's top line, above the heel counter, the shoe may have a dip in the center.

Heel lift

The heel lift of a shoe or shoe last is the dimension specified for the heel height above the ground. This is determined by the last of a shoe. A normal sports shoe will generally have a heel lift of 6 to 8mm above the ball of the foot. This is a standard ergonomic stance that will allow the shoe to have more cushioning under the heel. A casual shoe or sandal may have a lift of zero, and a high heel women's shoe last can have a heel lift of 4 inches or more.

Heel stabilizer

The heel stabilizer can be rubber, plastic, or leather. The stabilizer is bonded to the upper and midsole on the outside of the shoe as a functional and stylized part. Very common on the classic cut and buff style midsole type.

Insole

Footbed, or insole, is the foam padded mesh that your foot stands on. It may be removable or cemented in. The insole for high-end shoes will be molded EVA or PU foam. The insole for low-end shoes will be die-cut EVA.

Insole Board

A paper-based board used to provide structure inside a shoe. For example, a stiff hiking boot will have a thick plastic lasting board. Also called a sock liner.

Lace Loop

Usually made of nylon webbing. A very common way to attach laces. Also called a ghilly loop. This style can be sewn under the eyestay to make a hidden lace loop.

Lasting

Lasting is the operation that stretches the shoe upper over the foot form or last. Almost all shoes are lasted in some way. With the last inside the upper, the outsole can be bonded and pressed into place. Once the outsole is bonded, the shoe can be de-lasted. There are several types of lasting operations: slip lasting, board lasting, toe lasting, waist lasting, heel lasting, string lasting, California lasting, and hand lasting.

Lasting board

A fabric or paperboard sheet used to make the bottom of the shoe upper.

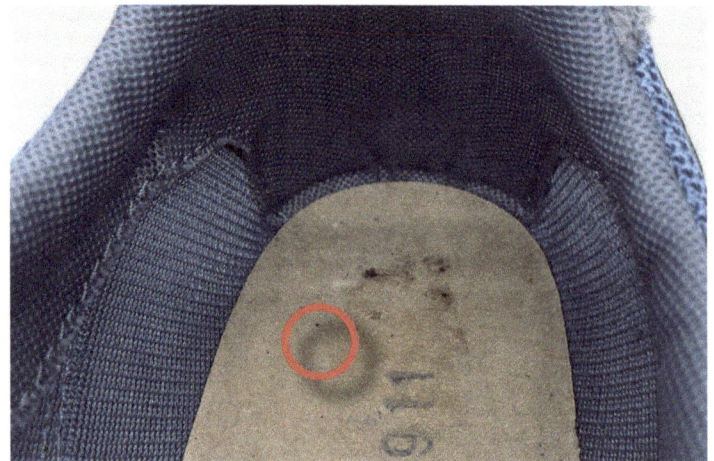

Lasting pressure

The lasting pressure is the amount of tension required to stretch the upper on the last form. Too much lasting pressure can damage, rip, or wrinkle the upper. Too little lasting pressure will result in a soft, ill-formed, baggy upper. It's up to the pattern master to get this right. Different materials will require different amounts of lasting pressure to look right.

Lateral side

The lateral side is the outside or the non-arched side of the shoe.

Linings of a shoe

1. Quarter Lining: horseshoe shape around back part of shoe
2. Vamp Lining: inside upper of forepart and toe of shoe
3. Sock Lining: covering all or part of the top surface of the insole.

Medial side

The medial side is the inside or arched side of the shoe. The outside is the lateral.

Midsole

The component of a shoe between the upper and outsole used to provide cushioning, fit, comfort, and support. Will be made of EVA or PU foam.

The shoe part: mudguard

The mudguard is the shoe pattern part along the forward part of the shoe along the edge of the outsole.

The shoe part: mustache

The mustache is the part attached to the shoe above the heel counter. The classic sneaker will have a mustache.

Outsole or sole unit

The bottom component of a shoe that provides grip and traction. The outsole is commonly rubber but can be high-density PU or EVA foam. Dress shoes may have leather bottoms.

Outsole channel stitch

The outsole will have a small groove or two molded into the rubber sidewall. After the shoe is assembled, a heavy-duty stitching machine with a special bent arm is used to stitch a heavy thread through the rubber sole and the upper of the shoe. This channel stitch is often used on the toe tip of joggers, the sidewall of skate shoes, and the bottoms of boat shoes.

Overlay

An upper part which is over another part. The Nike swoosh logo is an overlay part.

Padding

Refers to foam or other material, usually inside the collar or tongue, to add thickness/cushioning and improve fit. It is usually made of polyurethane, latex, EVA, or PE foam.

Parting line or outsole parting-plane

The line in an outsole mold is made by the closing edges of the tooling. The tooling is split at the parting line. A mold may have one or two parting planes. Extra rubber may spread out of the parting line; this will need to be trimmed off. A narrow, tight parting line or parting plane is a sign of quality tooling.

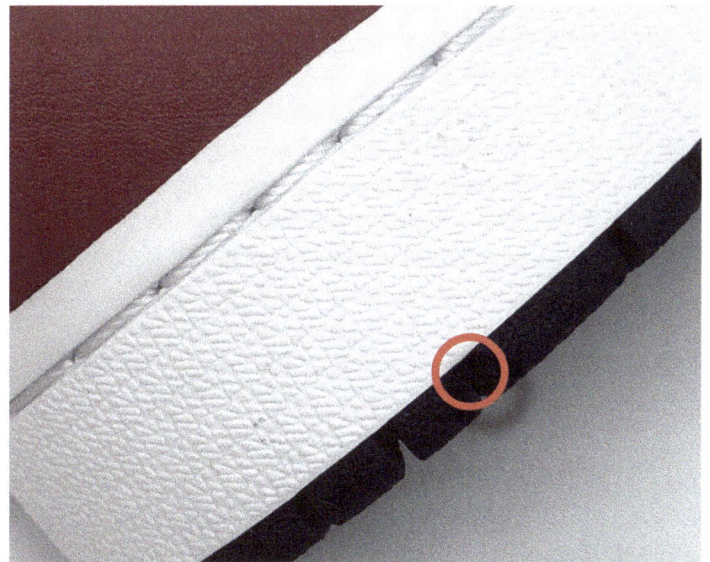

Pattern

The design of the shoe's cut parts. The shoe pattern is fit to the last. Designers and developers often make pattern corrections when creating a new shoe.

PU

Short for polyurethane. PU upper materials usually use a thin layer of PU foam with a non-woven or fabric backing for reinforcement and strength. PU can come in thousands of different colors and textures.

PU foam

Common padding inside shoe tongues and collars. Open cells allow air and water to enter. Can be very soft. Also known as KFF or K360 foam.

PU leather

A man-made material, often a composite made of two layers. A backing layer made of woven or non-woven polyester fibers combined with an external surface by "dry" lamination process or by "wet" liquid processes.

PU midsole foam

Another formulation of the Poly-Urethane material. In this case, foamed or blown into closed molds and used for midsoles, footbeds, and some upper cushioning parts. It can be heavier than EVA but is more elastic and bendable. Heavy-duty hiking shoes and work boots may have PU midsoles.

PU nubuck

A man-made material, often a composite made of two layers. A backing layer made of woven or non-woven polyester fibers combined with an external surface by "dry" lamination process. The top PU surface is slightly brushed to make a smooth matte finish. This is very common shoe material.

PVC leather

A man-made material often a composite made of two layers. A backing layer made of woven or non-woven polyester fibers, combined with an external surface by "dry" lamination process or by "wet" liquid processes.

The shoe part: quarter panel

The quarter panel is the main shoe pattern part on the side of the shoe. The Nike Swoosh, New Balance N, and the Vans V-Bar are all located on the quarter panel.

Sock or Sock liner

The sock, sock liner, footbed, or insole is the foam padded mesh on which your foot stands. It may be removable or may be cemented in. In high-end shoes, it will be made from molded EVA or PU foam. In low-end shoes, it will be made from die-cut EVA.

Split leather or suede leather

Split leather is the soft, hairy part of the animal hide. Suede is made by splitting the smooth surface off the top of the hide.

Stitch and turn (seam)

A seam that is stitched to join two parts, then flipped inside out, so the stitch is hidden. The stitch and turn seam is nearly always found where the shoe's collar meets the inner lining. This seam type is also used to hide material edges. To make the seam thinner, the edges are often skived before stitching, then the fabric may be hammered flat.

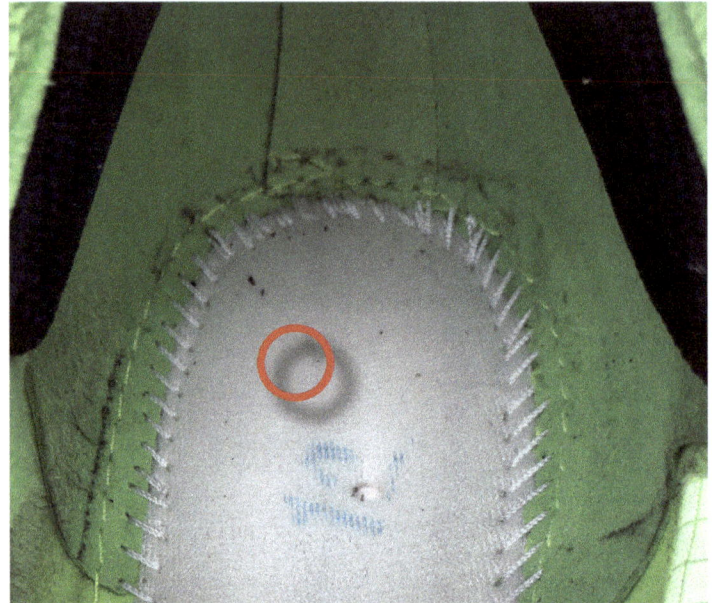

Strobel sock or Strobel board

The Strobel is the fabric or non-woven material used to finish the bottom of a shoe upper. The worker uses a Strobel machine to make a Strobel stitch to attach the Strobel board to the upper. It was invented by a guy named Strobel.

Suede leather or split leather

Suede leather is leather created from the fibrous part of the hide left once the top-grain of the raw hide has been separated from the hide. During the splitting operation, the top grain and drop split are separated. Suede is "fuzzy" on both sides.

Super tuff

Super tuff is a very common, non-woven reinforcement material, found in all types of shoes. You will find super tuff behind punched holes and metal hardware.

Synthetic leather

Man-made material, often a composite made of two layers. A backing layer made of woven or non-woven polyester fibers combined with an external surface by "dry" lamination process or by "wet" liquid processes.

Throat of the shoe
The shoe's throat is the opening where the shoe tongue is attached and is spanned by the laces. The throat is generally surrounded by the shoe's eyestay.

Toe box
The toe area of the shoe. Different styles will have different toe box sizes and shapes. Fashion shoes may have tight, pointed tips while work boots have extra space for steel toe inserts.

Toe puff
Toe puff is the reinforcing material used to hold the shape of the toe box. It can be thermoplastic, which is easily shaped with heat, leather, or fabric. It also comes in many styles, from soft to firm.

Toe spring
The toe spring of a last, shoe, or pattern is simply how much the front tip is off the ground. A stiff hiking boot may have a 15mm toe spring, while a slip-on casual shoe may have a 5mm toe spring. As a general rule, the stiffer the shoe sole, the more toe spring you need for a normal rolling stride.

Toe tip
The pattern part on the front of the shoe. Usually reinforced.

Top line
The top edge of the shoe's ankle opening.

Tread or shoe tread
The part of the shoe that contacts the ground. The shoe tread is most commonly made of rubber.

Vamp
The vamp is the area on top of the toes. The vamp is often made from breathable mesh or has perforations for venting.

Vulcanize
The process of heating raw rubber to cure it. This process creates crosslinks inside the rubber compound, bonding it together. Before the rubber is vulcanized, it is stretchable, gummy, and easy to tear. After being vulcanized, it's tough and ready to wear.

Wedge or midsole wedge
The EVA foam midsole of a shoe, thinner in the front and taller in the heel. When you use the word "wedge," you are usually referring to a die-cut midsole part.

Chapter 4 : How to Inspect a Sneaker

Quality Inspections: How to inspect a sneaker like a pro
Once you learn how to professionally inspect a pair of shoes, you will never look at them the same way again. Quality is a very important feature for any pair of shoes you may authenticate, buy, sell, or make.

Knowing how to run a shoe quality inspection is a critical skill for shoe traders, designers, developers, and product line managers. When a sneaker arrives, it is critical to inspect the materials, assembly technique, and workmanship. Inspecting a sneaker is a great skill to have as a shoe buying customer in a store. Here is how to grade and inspect a shoe like a professional.

Fake shoes are cheap shoes
Fake shoes all have one common flaw. They are made cheaply and quickly. The counterfeiting shoe factories will skip any expensive components or difficult production processes. Hidden components like internal airbags or carbon shank plates are left off. The counterfeiting factory will not waste time using the shaping machines to heat and remold the heel counters and toe reinforcements. The fake shoes won't have the same side profile, and they won't fit like the authentic shoe.

Human hands
All shoes are made by human hands, so even an experienced and careful worker at a top Nike shoe factory can have a bad day and make a mistake. You will find that a shoe 100% proven to be made by Nike can have quality flaws. If you are shopping in a store, just ask for a different pair. You would never buy a new car with scratched paint, right? So don't settle for less when buying new shoes.

In this chapter, you will learn how to judge a shoe. Your eyes and hands are the only tools you will need.

Definition of shoe inspection quality "A," "B," "C" grades:

"A" grade shoes:
Shoes without any functional or cosmetic defects to impair the marketability of the shoe. High-quality shoes which look good and fit correctly. An A grade must follow the production specifications and match the approved confirmation sample.

"B" grade shoes:
Shoes without any major functional defects that could cause injury to the person wearing the shoes. These shoes may have cosmetic defects, production mistakes, or workmanship issues that cannot be properly repaired. These will be discounted or diverted to markets more tolerant of cosmetic defects.

"C" grade shoes:
These shoes have major functional defects that could cause injury to the wearer or major cosmetic defects that cannot be repaired. Shoes are also considered C-grade if they have poor workmanship or material defects that could shorten the normal life expectancy of the shoe, or damage the company's reputation. C-grade shoes should be destroyed.

How to inspect a shoe

The main points of an inspection are as follows:
#1. Is this the correct shoe, a matched pair?
#2. Is the shoe clean?
#3. Does the shoe follow the specification?
#4. Is the workmanship of high quality?
#5. Is the shoe damaged in any way?

Let's inspect a shoe!

The first step in any inspection is to review the shoe packaging.

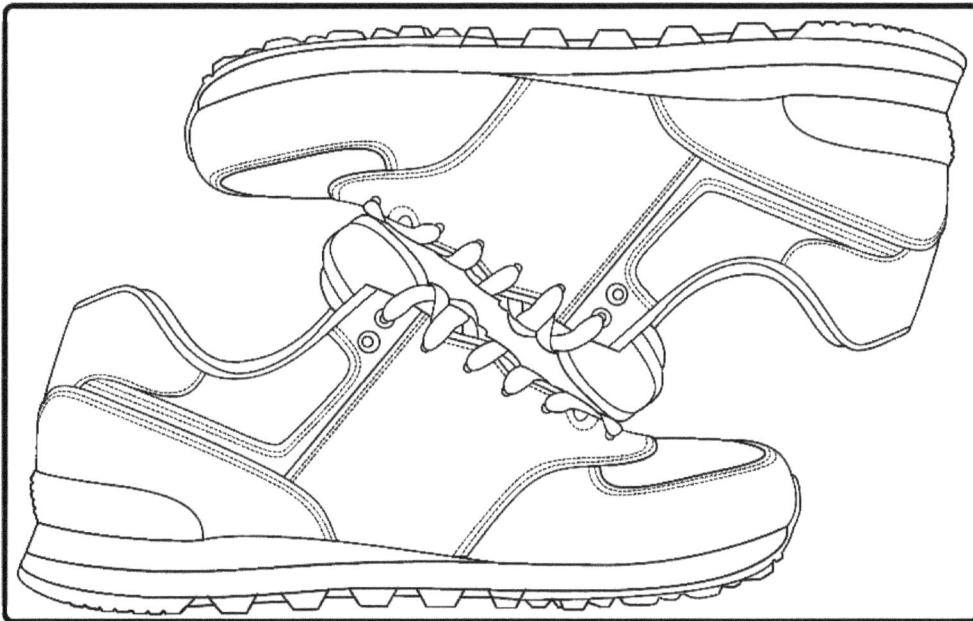

Is the shoe in the correct inner box for its model?
Is the box presentable? Make sure the box is not damaged or dirty.
Is the box the correct size? The shoes should not be crushed inside a too small box.

Confirm the information on the box end label matches the shoe's color, model, and size.
Check any hangtags to ensure they are correct for the shoe.

Do you have a left and right?

Remove the shoes from the packing box.
Are the shoes the same size and color?
Check the shoe tongue label information.
In the factory, it's easy to mistakenly put a right
size 7 and a left size 7.5 into the same box.

Holding the pair of shoes, place the shoes bottom
to bottom.

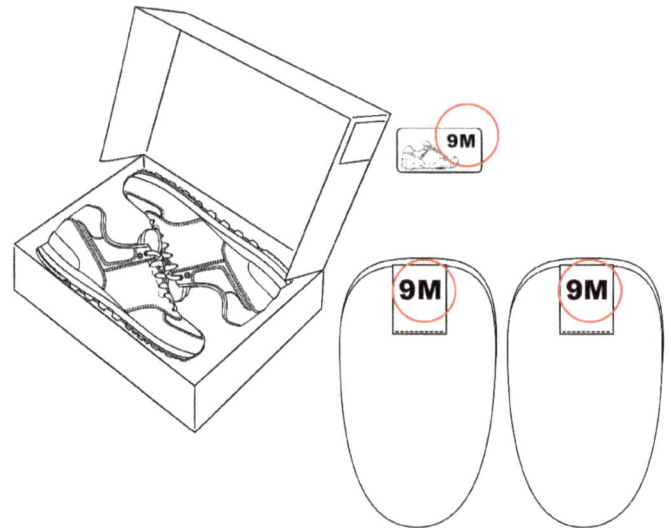

Check for symmetry

Does the pair match in length? The size marks
may match up, but check that the shoes are in
fact the same length.

Now, holding the shoe from the bottom, roll the
uppers together side by side.
You are checking the alignment of the shoe parts.
Starting from the front, roll the shoes to align
the parts: toe caps, vamps, overlays, eye stays,
eyelets.

While you have the uppers side by side, compare
the finish and colors of each part.

Next, hold the shoes up, looking at the heels.
Make sure the shoe sits on the outsole straight.
Check that the upper is not rotated off-center.

Next, rolling the heels together, check that the
back height and collar lines match.

Study the shoe bottoms. Do they match? Are the
color blocks in the same location? Look over the
midsole sidewall for wrinkles. Check the seam
joining the upper to the outsole. Look for any
extra glue on the upper, 2mm is the limit for "over
gluing." Look for over buffing of the upper.
On the shoe bottom, check for color bleeding
between color blocks. Look for any paint covering
mistakes. Check to make sure the outsole parts fit
together neatly without any extra glue.

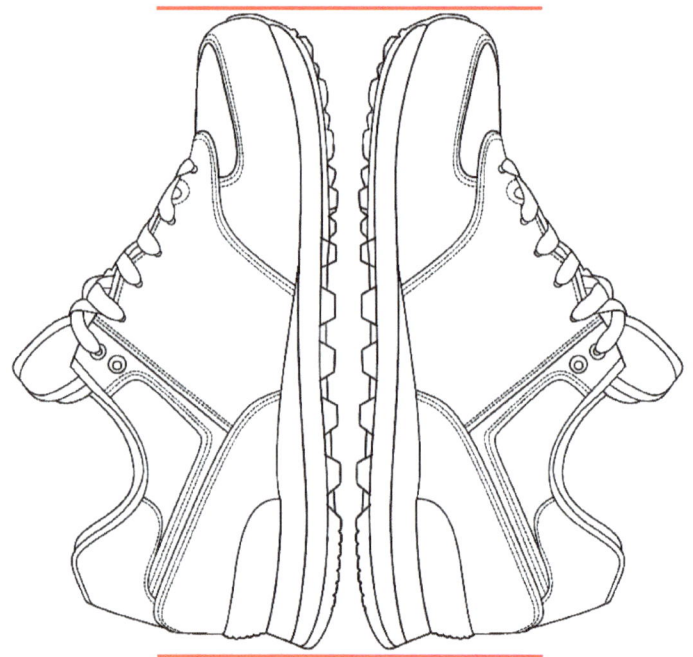

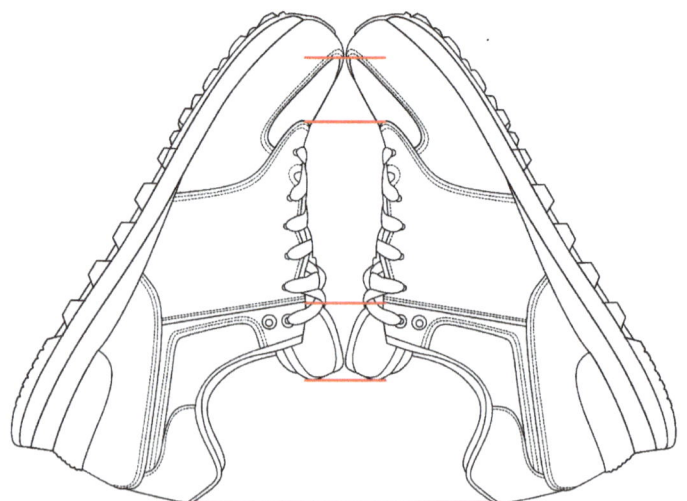

Colors and materials

While you have the uppers side by side, compare the finish and colors of each part and compare the left to the right.

With suede shoes the leather color from shoe to shoe may not match. For full grain leather shoes, study the emboss pattern to make sure the parts have the same texture. If the leather or mesh parts have a direction to the surface emboss, check that the pattern runs in the same direction.

Stitching

Next, look over the stitching. You don't want to see loose or broken stitches. Be on the lookout for melted stitch ends. The shoe factory will use a heat gun to melt off loose thread ends, this can leave a small fused ball of melted plastic behind. Double and single needle stitch lines are often mixed on fake shoes. Compare the left and right to make sure they match.

Look and feel inside

Now that we looked over the outside, it's time to dive inside. A great looking shoe with defects inside is not saleable.

Look inside the shoe opening. Is the lining clean and free of wrinkles? Make sure the footbed is straight, level, and fits correctly. If the footbed is too small, it may slide around, too big and the footbed may wrinkle or curl.

Is the collar lining clean and without wrinkles? Run your hand around the collar, feel for any lumps, bumps, or glue. Next, run your hand down inside. Feel around the edges of the footbed for wrinkles or channel stitching defects.

Check the edges of the tongue for rough stitching or creases in the edges. Make sure to feel where the tongue is attached to the bottom of the shoe's throat. This area can have rough stitching or a hard lump if the foam is not trimmed from the base of the tongue.

Make sure to reach all the way down into the vamp and toe tip. You are feeling for wrinkles in the front edge of the footbed and any rough stitching.

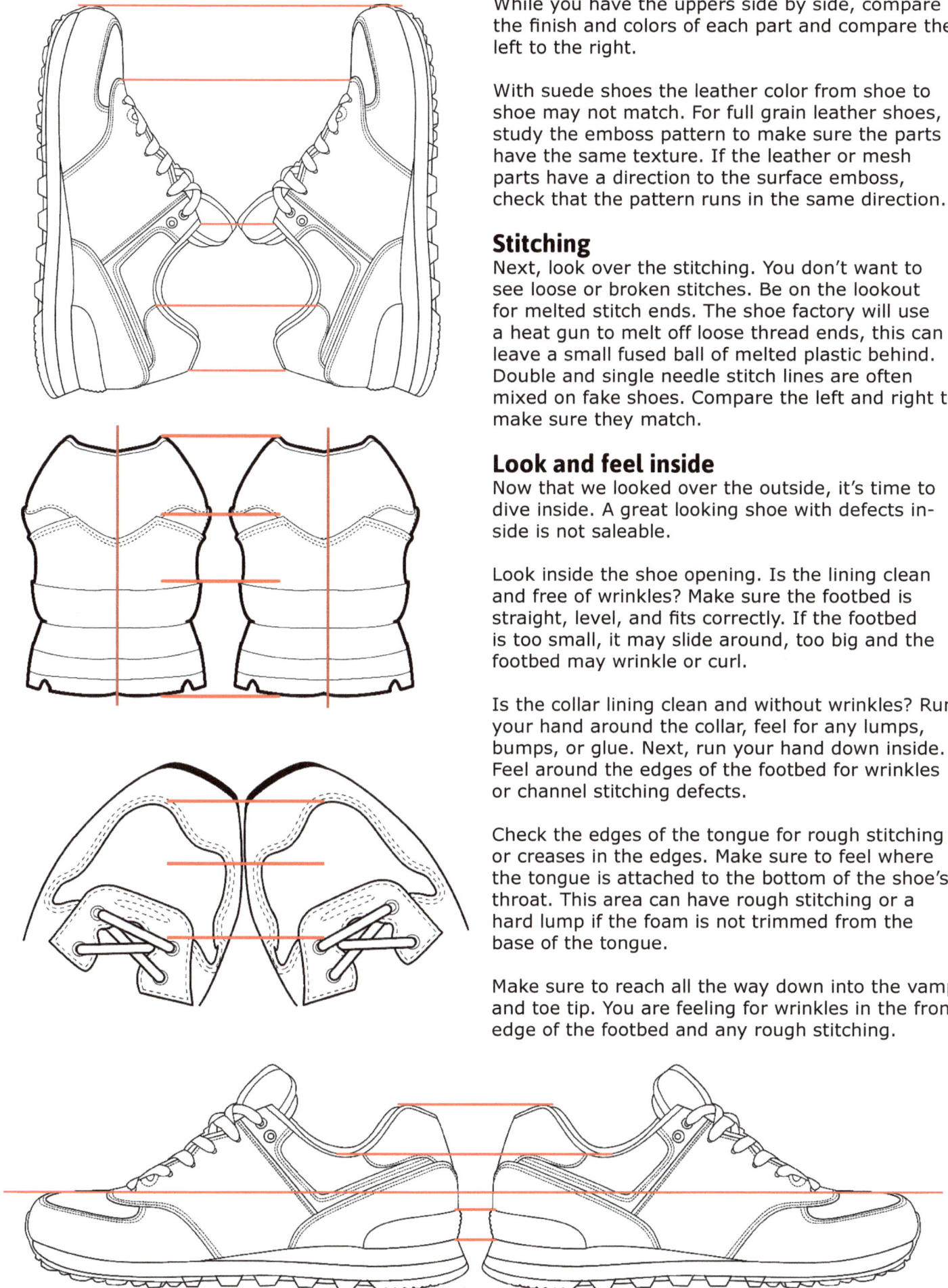

24

Common shoe quality problems

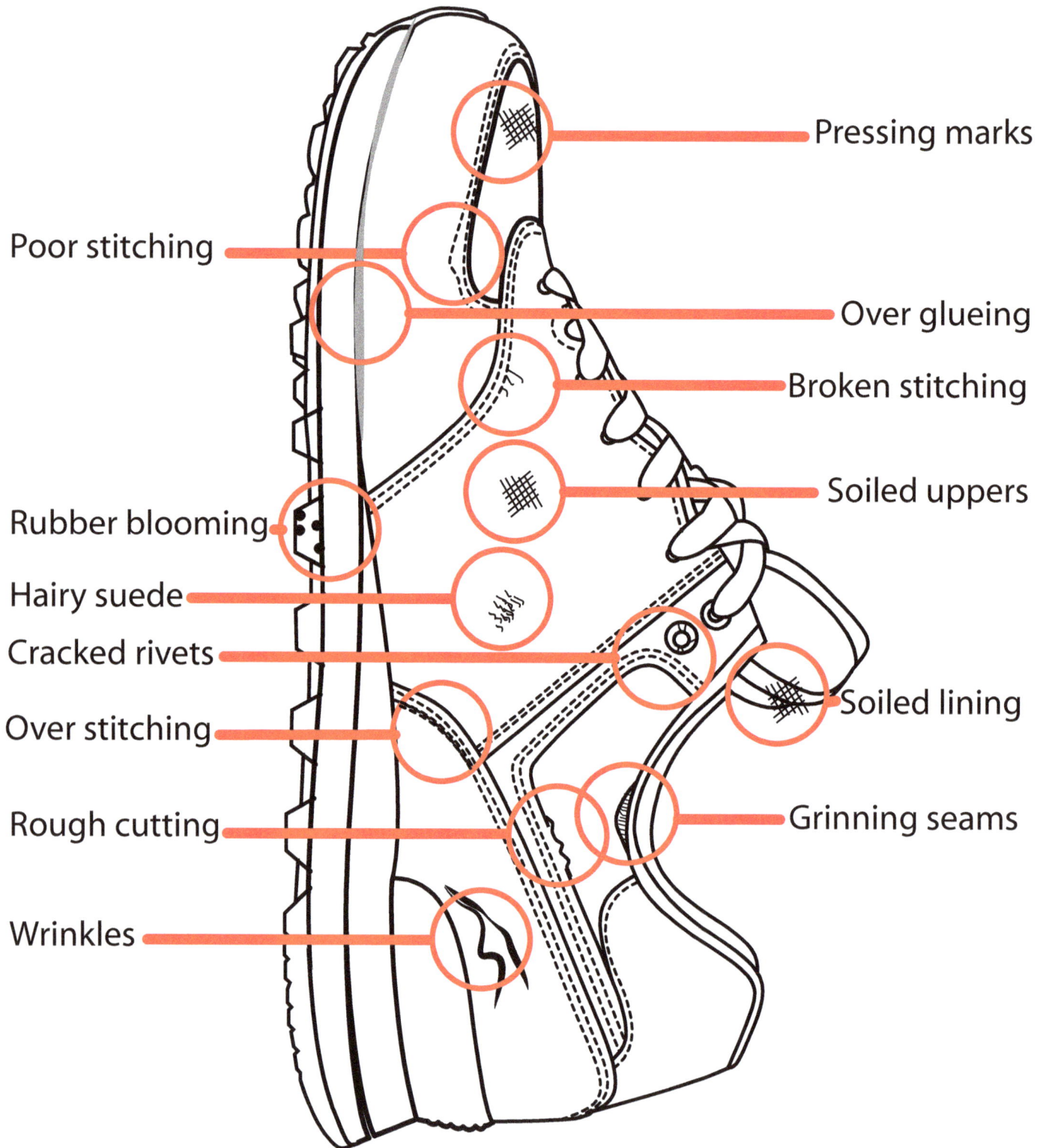

Pressing marks

Poor stitching

Over glueing

Broken stitching

Soiled uppers

Rubber blooming

Hairy suede

Cracked rivets

Soiled lining

Over stitching

Rough cutting

Grinning seams

Wrinkles

Systematic quality

When inspecting, it's critical to decide if any problems you see are a one-time mistake or a systematic problem that will effect every shoe. Remember, inside every factory, each operation is done by the same worker. If the vamp stitcher is having a bad day, you may see lots of crooked stitching on a vamp.

If you are inspecting "inbound" shoes inside your warehouse, you already own the problem. Ask yourself, "How did this shoe get this far? Who missed these problems inside the factory before the shoes shipped?" Heads should be rolling. Your factory has a QC system flaw. Can you "fix" your factory? Maybe you need to find a new one?

Common shoe quality problems

When inspecting a shoe, there are common things you should be looking for:

Are the shoes clean?
Clean shoes can be hard to make in a dirty factory.

Do the colors match?
Suede and natural leathers can be tricky to match.

How is the material quality?
Check for hairy suede or other material issues.

Is the cutting clean?
Check that the trim and cut edges are not rough.

Are there wrinkles in the upper?
Check around the collar foam.

How is the stitching?
Check for crooked or broken stitches and stitch holes without stitches.

Do you see any pressing marks on the vamp?

Are there any dirty or smeared logos?

Did you review the seams?
If you can see the stitches, this is called "grinning."

How is the lasting quality?
Over lasting can pull seams near the toe apart or cause wrinkles.

Is there any rubber blooming?
Look for white film on the rubber parts.

Do you see the rubber color bleeding?

How are the tongues attached? Check that they are not crooked and are attached at the same height.
Do you see any wrinkles on the foam parts?

Did you check for over gluing?
Glue should not extend more than 2mm above the outsole edge.

Are there signs of over buffing?
Buffing should not extend more than 2mm above the outsole edge.

Is there under gluing? Look for dry spots along the sole without glue.

Did you review the outsole?
Check for any outsole parts splitting, cupped, bowed, or crooked.

Rubber blooming - chemicals inside the rubber are leaching out.

Rough cutting caused by dull cutting dies.

Rough stitching caused by poor workmanship.

26

Color bleeding over the outsole parting line. The shoe is also dirty. There is a little over gluing on the outsole.

Painted rubber. Unstable rubber is yellowing in UV light.

Rough stitching, not following the edge

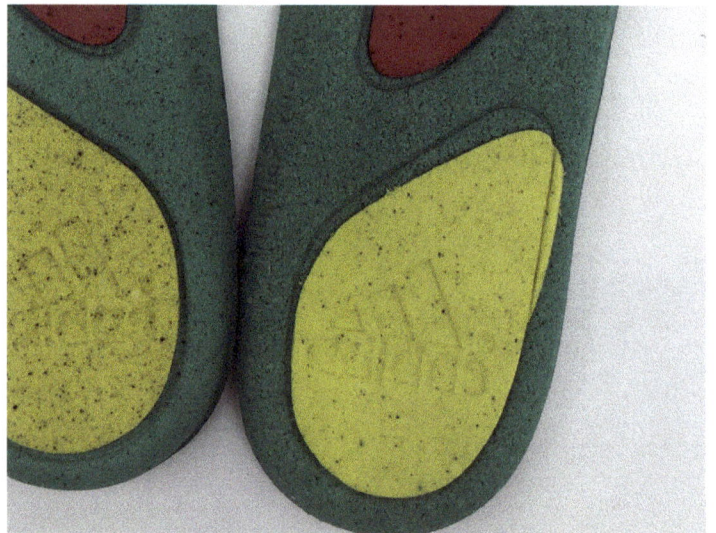

Color bleeding. The foam insert is not fitting in it's space.

Poorly turned seam is lumpy and mis-shapen.

Low quality hairy "belly" suede. Belly suede stretches and splits.

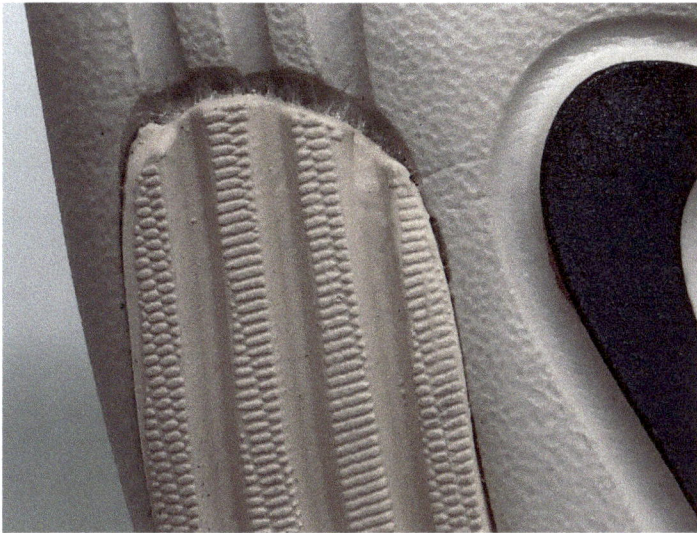

Parts don't fit together, cheap molds and poor stock fitting.

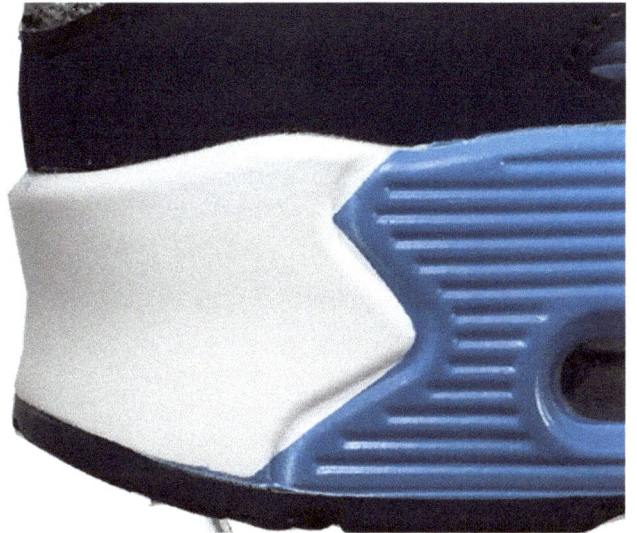

Rushed paint work.

Backing foam is too soft and causing wrinkles.

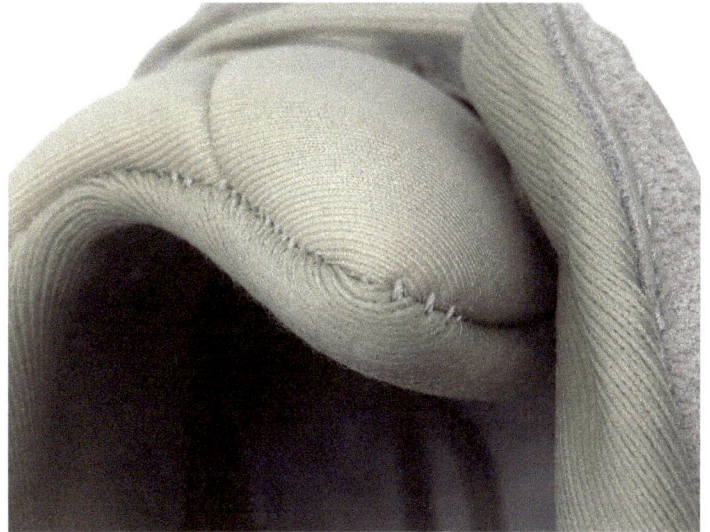

Turned out seams with stitching showing

Upper is twisted or "clocked" during lasting operation.

Wrinkles and mis-shaped heel counter are proof of being improperly molded.

Complete Shoe Inspection Checklist

Check the packaging

1. Is the shoe in the correct inner box for its model?
2. Is the box presentable? Make sure the box is not damaged or dirty.
3. Is the box the correct size? The shoes should not be crushed or loose inside.
4. Does the information on the box end label match with the shoe's color, model, and size?
5. Check any hangtags to ensure they are correct for the shoe.
6. Do you have a left and right shoe?
7. Are the shoes the same size and color?
8. Check the tongue label information to ensure it matches with the shoes.

Check the uppers for symmetry

1. Does the pair match in length? If the size marks agree, confirm the shoes are the same length.
2. Roll the uppers together side by side, checking the alignment of the shoe parts.
3. Do the toe caps, vamps, overlays, eye stays, eyelets all match up?
4. How are the tongues attached? Are they straight? Are they attached at the same height?
5. Hold the shoes up and look at the heels. Make sure the shoe sits on the outsole straight.
6. Check that the upper is not rotated or clocked off-center.
7. Roll the heels together, check that the back height and collar lines match.

Check the materials for defects

1. With the uppers side by side, compare the finish and colors of each shoe part.
2. Do the colors match? Examine them piece by piece. Check the backing colors.
3. If the leather or mesh parts have a surface emboss, do the patterns run in the same direction?
4. Look over the stitching. You don't want to see loose or broken stitches.
5. Are the stick lines neat, smooth, and do they follow the edge of the parts closely?
6. Do the stitching patterns match? Single stitch lines, double stitch lines, and triple stitch lines.
7. Be on the lookout for melted stitch ends.
8. Do the thread colors match?
9. Check for hairy suede or other material issues or mismatched backing colors.
10. Are the cut edges clean?
11. Look at any rolled edges and check that they are smooth and even.
12. Check that binding edges are smooth with even edge exposure.
13. Do you see any pressing marks on the vamp?
14. Are there dirty or smeared logos? Check embroidery logos for dirt or snagged stitches.
15. Did you review the seams? If you see the stitches, this issue is called "grinning."
16. Look for X-ray issues where overlays or seams are showing from underneath.
17. Check metal hardware for scratches or chips. Make sure rivet backs are smooth, not cracked.
18. Are the aglets smooth, straight, and stiff? They should not be bent or cracked.
19. Are the shoelaces the same length, color-matched, and free of snags or glue?

Check the outsoles

1. Do the shoe bottoms match? Are the color blocks in the same location?
2. Look over the midsole sidewall for wrinkles.
3. Examine the seam joining the upper to the outsole.
4. Look for any extra glue on the upper; 2mm is the limit for over gluing.
5. Look for over buffing of the upper.
6. On the shoe bottom, check for color bleeding between color blocks.
7. Look for any paint which may be covering mistakes.
8. Check to make sure the outsole parts fit together neatly without any extra glue.
9. Check for outsole parts that may be splitting, cupped, bowed, or crooked.
10. Is there any rubber blooming? Look for chalky white film on the rubber parts.
11. Do the shoes sit flat?
12. Does the toe spring match on the left and right foot?

Check inside the shoes

1. Look inside the shoe opening. Is the lining clean and free of wrinkles?
2. Make sure the footbed is straight, level, and fits correctly. An oversized footbed may wrinkle or curl.
3. Is the collar lining clean and wrinkle-free?
4. Run your hand around the collar, feel for any lumps, bumps, or glue.
5. Feel around the edges of the footbed for wrinkles or channel stitching defects.
6. Check the edges of the tongue for rough stitching or creases in the edges.
7. Make sure to feel where the tongue is attached to the bottom of the shoe's throat.
   This area can have rough stitching or a hard lump.
8. Make sure to reach all the way down into the vamp and toe tip.
   You are feeling for wrinkles in the front edge of the footbed and any rough stitching.

Check the fit and function

1. Are the uppers too stiff or too flexible for the function of the shoe?
2. Is the sole too stiff or too soft per the function of the shoe?

Chapter 5 : How to Inspect The Vans Old Skool

In this chapter, we are going to practice our sneaker inspection skills with a pair of classic Vans Old Skool vulcanized shoes. Here at the SneakerFactory.net, we really like Vans. They offer great shoes, and we know the guys that make them. However, shoes are made by people, and people can make mistakes. So let's get started with our Vans Old Skool inspection.

The Vans Old Skool provenance

We mail-ordered these shoes directly from Vans to ensure they are authentic Old Skool sneakers and not fake Vans. Regardless, when a new shoe arrives it is critical to inspect the materials, assembly technique, and workmanship. To do this, you must know the correct footwear inspection procedure. As a buyer of shoes for personal use, it's nice to run your own inspection on the shoes before you buy them.

How to inspect The Vans Old Skool

Inspect the Vans inner box

The first step in any inspection is to review the shoe packaging. The "inner" box is the box that is inside the case packing. What consumers think of as "the shoe box" is really the inner box.

Is the shoe in the correct inner box for its model?
Is the box presentable?
Make sure the box is not damaged or dirty.
Is the box the correct size?

The shoes should not be crushed inside a box that is too small. Counterfeiters usually skip the box, if they do include the box it will be thin cardboard and easy to crush and wrinkle. Look for spelling errors on any printed materials.

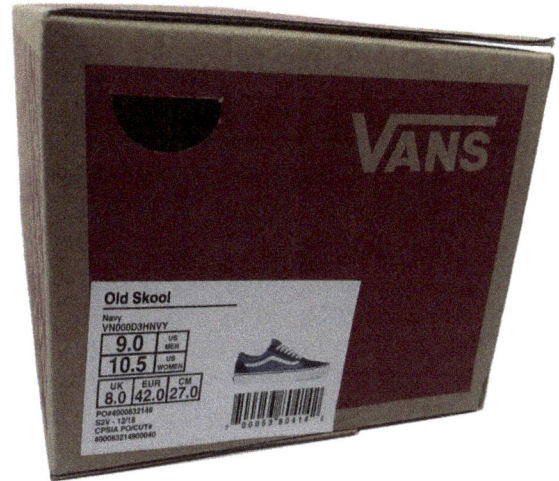

Is this the correct shoe

Confirm the information on the box end label matches the shoe's color, model, and size.
Check any hangtags to ensure they are correct for the shoe. In the case of Vans shoes, look for the "OFF THE WALL" tag. It will be die-cut to the shape of a skate board.

Let's inspect a shoe

Remove the Vans from the packing box.
Are the shoes the same size and suede color?
Check the shoe tongue label information.
In the factory, the shoes will be packed by the hundreds per hour. It's not hard to put a right size 7 and a left size 7.5 into the same box. Or even two lefts.

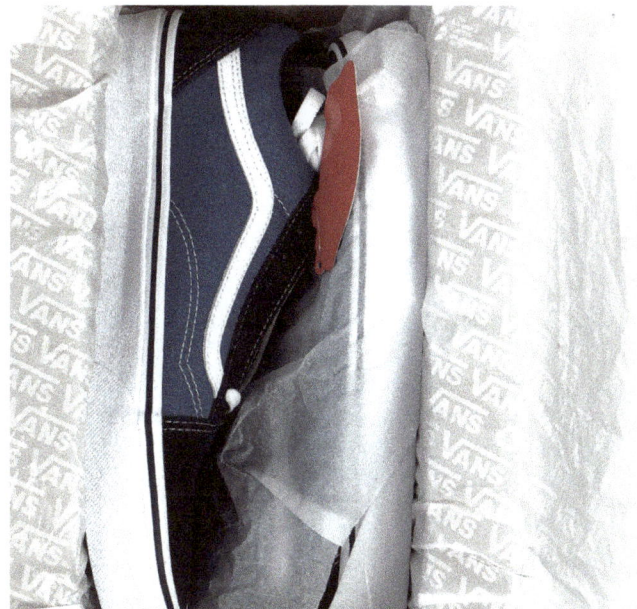

Do you have a left and a right?

Yes, it sounds crazy, but sometimes you will find a mismatched pair of shoes. The shoes are made in pairs, but in the final packing operations, lefts and rights can get mixed up. Remember, if you buy shoes from a store, you may not be the first person to try them on.

First checks

Before we dig deeper into the quality inspection, it's a good idea to give the shoe a quick once over to see if it is really in new, unworn condition. Is the shoe clean? Check the bottom for wear and the upper for any smudges or dirt.

You can put your nose to work too. The Vans vulcanized construction shoes should have a strong rubber smell, not a glue smell.

Checking for symmetry

Does the pair of shoes match in length? The size marks may match up, but check that the shoes are, in fact, the same length. Check the length by holding the shoes bottom to bottom.

Check the uppers by rolling the shoes

Now, holding the Vans from the bottom, roll the uppers together side by side.

As you roll the shoes together, you are checking the alignment of the shoe parts. Starting from the toe tip, roll the shoes to align the parts: toe caps, vamps, overlays, eye stays, eyelets.

Roll the shoes to a side by side position. Look at each part to make sure they match and are in the correct position.

Colors and materials

While you have the uppers side by side, compare the finish and colors of each part and compare the left to the right.

With suede shoes, the leather color from shoe to shoe may not match. For full grain leather shoes, study the emboss pattern to make sure the parts have the same texture. If the leather or mesh parts have a direction to the surface emboss, check that the pattern runs in the same direction.

Heels and top lines

Make sure the shoe sits on the outsole straight. Place the shoes on a smooth flat surface and check that the soles sit flat and the uppers are straight.

Check that the upper is not rotated off-center. The Old Skool has a contrasting color back seam you can use as a guide. The center-line of the shoe should be straight up. Board lasted shoes can be twisted, crooked, or rocked forward. Check the heel heights to confirm they are the same.

This is a good time to look at the heel counter shape. A correctly molded heel counter will have a slightly convex or outwardly cupped contour. This shoe has the ideal "hourglass" shape. The Vans shoes will have a soft rubber heel counter; it should flex easily.

Next, rolling the heels together, check that the back height and collar lines match.

Vulcanized outsoles

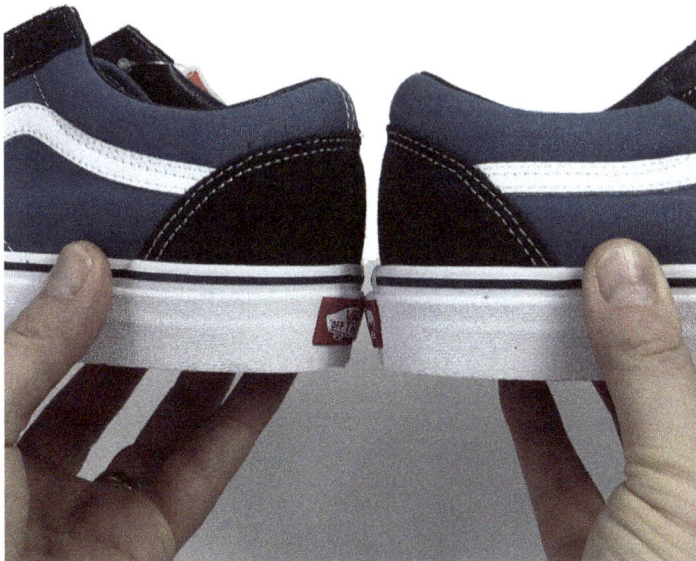

Stitching

Next, look over the stitching. You don't want to see loose or broken stitches. Be on the look out for melted stitch ends. The shoe factory will use a heat gun to melt off loose thread ends, this can leave a small fused ball of melted plastic behind. Double and single needle stitch lines are often mixed on fake shoes. Compare the left and right to make sure they match.

Because the Old Skool has contrast colored stitching, it's easy to see any stitching flaws.

34

Vans footwear inspection: look inside!

To complete your Vans Old Skool inspection, you need to check each shoe inside and out. Now that we looked outside, it's time to dive inside. A great looking shoe with defects inside is not saleable.

Look inside the shoe opening, is the lining clean and free of wrinkles? For Vans skate shoes, make sure the footbed is straight, level, and fitting correctly. If the footbed is too small, it may slide around, too big and the footbed may wrinkle or curl.

Look inside the Old Skool opening, is the lining clean and without wrinkles?

Run your hand around the collar, feel for any lumps, bumps, or glue. Next, run your hand down inside. Feel around the edges of the footbed for any wrinkles or channel stitching defects.

Check the edges of the tongue for rough stitching or creases. Make sure to feel where the tongue is attached to the bottom of the shoe's throat. This area can have rough stitching or a hard lump if the foam is not trimmed from the base of the tongue.

Make sure to reach all the way down into the vamp and toe tip. Feel for any wrinkles in the front edge of the footbed and any rough stitching.

Study the waffle bottoms. Do they match? Look over the foxing sidewall tape for wrinkles. Check the seam joining the upper to the outsole. Look for extra glue on the upper; 2mm is the limit for "over gluing." Look for over buffing of the upper.

Check that the shoe sits flat on its bottom. Is the sole flat? Check for any soft spots on the bottom of the sole. Soft spots are evidence the inside of the shoe is not securely glued together.

The Vans vulcanized sole construction results in a soft and very flexible sole. The bottom waffle pattern is likely to be cupped. While this is not great quality, it is authentic to the classic design and construction technique.

Final words on Vans Old Skool inspection

When inspecting, it's critical to decide if the problems you see are a "one-off" mistake or a systematic problem that will affect every shoe? It's very important to understand that inside the factory, the same worker completes one operation on every shoe. If the vamp stitcher is having a bad day, you may see lots of crooked stitching on a vamp.

Some hairy suede and rough cutting, not great, but this is still an A grade Vans Old Skool.

Yes, this looks horrible, but this is a Vans trademark feature. The foxing tape overlap with heel bump is correct.

The trimmed edge of the rubber is difficult to make 100% clean. This is the charm of vulcanized construction. Again, a typical "flaw" or "feature" of this construction technique and an authentic Vans Old Skool sneaker.

Are Vans good shoes?

Yes! Vans shoes are well made, and Vans uses high-quality materials. Vans is one division of the huge $14 billion VF Corporation.

Vans is just one of the many footwear brands controlled by VF. These brands include North Face, Timberland, Smartwool, Icebreaker, Altra, Napapijri, Kipling, Eastpak, JanSport, Reef, Eagle Creek, Dickies, Red Kap, Bulwark, Timberland, Kodiak, and Horace Small.

The point here is that Vans has all the people, expertise, and capital to make great shoes.

38

Chapter 6 : How to Inspect The Nike Air Jordan 1 Mid OG

The Nike Air Jordan 1 is one of the most collected shoes in the sneaker market. This makes it the biggest target for sneaker counterfeiters. Nike has produced millions of pairs in hundreds of different colors and configurations. The many authentic variations in color and materials make it difficult to know if a particular colorway is a "real" Nike product. Still, we have a great tool to detect fakes.

That tool is our compete quality inspection!

The Air Jordan provenance
We mail-ordered these shoes directly from StockX to ensure they are authentic Nike sneakers. You will see in the course of this inspection that no shoe is perfect. Even this 100% real shoe made by Nike still has flaws. But, you will see these flaws are individual to this pair of shoes and not due to counterfeiting.

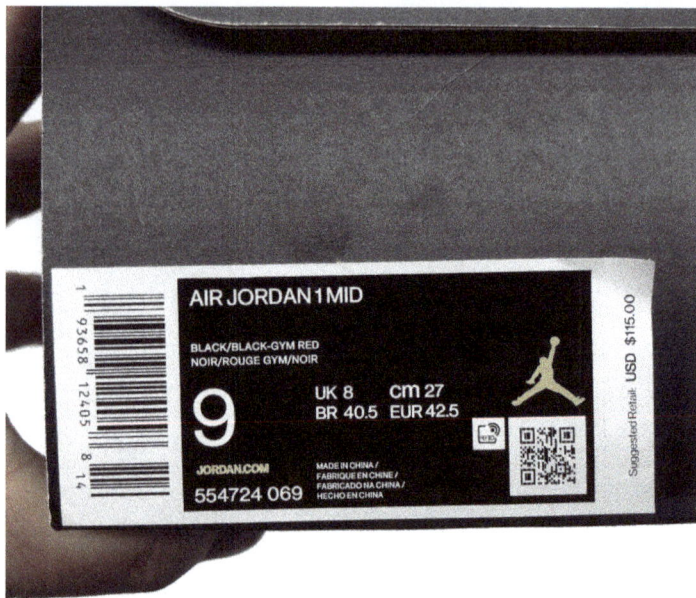

How to inspect The Air Jordan Mid

Check the inner box
The first step in any inspection is to review the shoe packaging. The "inner box" is the box inside the case packing. The box most consumers think of as the shoe box is really the inner box.

Is the shoe in the correct inner box for its model? Is the box presentable? Make sure the box is not damaged or dirty. Is the box the correct size? The shoes should not be crushed inside a box that is too small. Counterfeiters usually skip the box. If they do include a box it will be thin cardboard and easy to crush and wrinkle. Look for spelling errors on any printed materials.

Is this the correct shoe?
Confirm the information on the box end label matches the shoe's color, model, and size. Check any hangtags to ensure they are correct for the shoe.

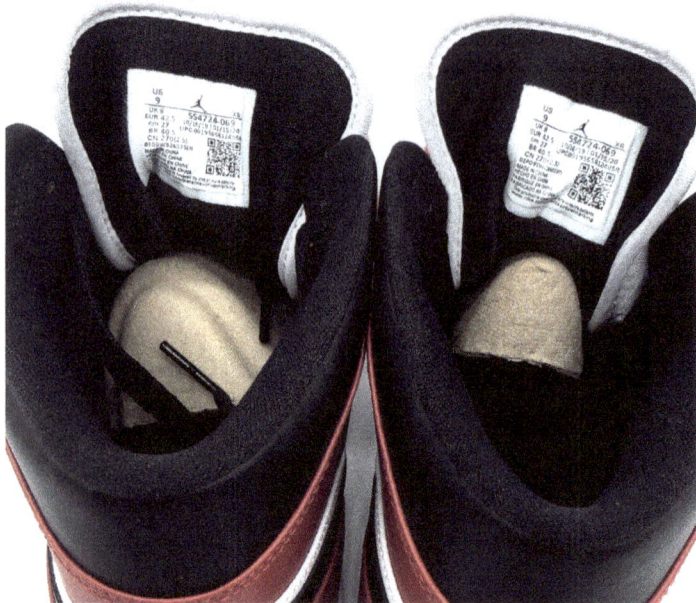

Let's inspect a shoe
Remove the shoes from the packing box.
Are the shoes the same size and color?
Check the shoe tongue label information.
In the factory, it's not hard to put a right size 7 and a left size 7.5 into the same box.

Do you have a left and a right?
Yes, it sounds crazy but sometimes you will find a mismatched pair of shoes. The shoes are made in pairs but in the final packing operations lefts and rights can get mixed up. Remember, if you buy shoes from a store, you may not be the first person to try them on.

Holding the pair of shoes, place the shoes bottom to bottom.

First checks
Before we dig deeper into the quality inspection, it is a good idea to give the shoe the quick once over to see if the shoe is in new, unworn condition. Are the shoes clean? Check the bottoms for wear and the uppers for any smudges or dirt.

You can put your nose to work too. If the shoe smells damp or musty, it may already have mold growing. If a shoe was packed or stored in damp conditions, it could have a funky smell.

Nike has switched to water-based and low VOC cements, so if you are hit with an overpowering "new shoe smell," you may have a fake shoe made with cheap, smelly glue.

Packing details

We can take the time to review some of the packing details. For example, do the bar codes scan? Does the UPC match the box label?

Do the shoes come with logo printed tissue paper? Is the logo spelled correctly?

Looking at the shoe stuffer, we see the Nike last code is molded into the paper. Nike uses the letter "Q" on their lasts.

Turn the box over; in this case, we can see the gold foil logo emboss. Not many counterfeiters will spend time copying that detail.

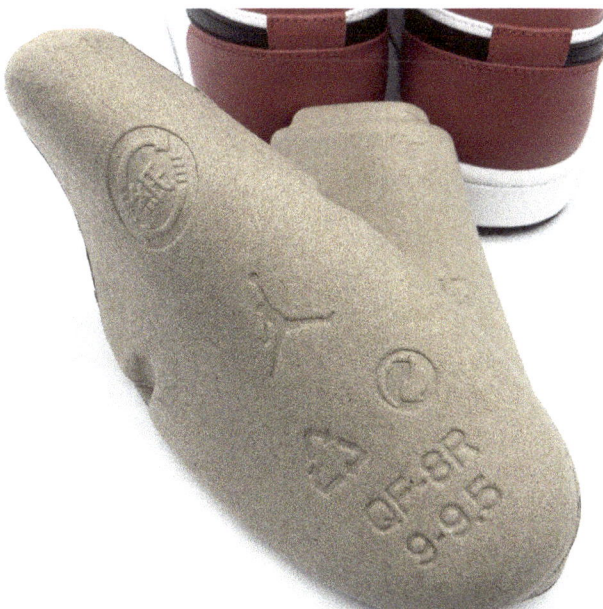

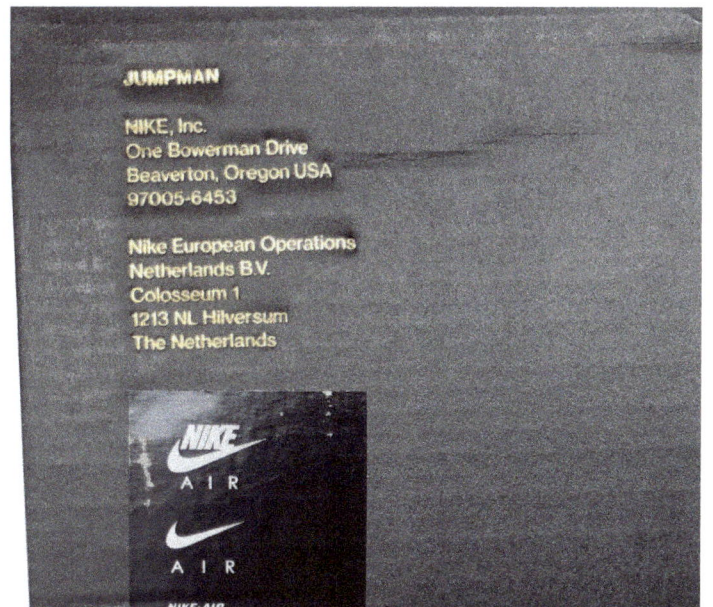

42

Check for symmetry

Does the pair match in length? The size marks may match up, but check that the shoes are in fact, the same length.

Roll the shoes

Now, holding the shoes from the bottom, roll the uppers together side by side.

As you roll the shoes together, you are checking the alignment of the shoe parts. Starting from the front, roll the shoes to align the parts: toe caps, vamps, overlays, eye stays, eyelets.

Roll the shoes to a side by side position. Look at each part to make sure they match and are in the correct position.

43

Heels and top lines

Make sure the shoe sits on the outsole straight. Place the shoes on a smooth, flat surface and check that the soles sit flat and the uppers are straight.

Check that the upper is not rotated off-center. The center line of the shoe should be straight up. Stobel shoes can be "twisted" or "clocked" on the last.

This is a good time to look at the heel counter shape. A correctly molded heel counter will have a slightly convex or outwardly cupped contour. This shoe has the ideal "hour glass" shape.

Next, rolling the heels together, check that the back height and collar lines match.

Symmetry is a signal of a high-quality shoe.

Topline contour

With the shoes heel to heel, study the topline contours. In this case, we can see the logo panel overlays are perfectly straight, but the rolled top line seam is a little wavy on the left side.

This is a minor flaw, the wave in the rolled topline edge is due to the inside stitch line being off center, or the lining was not completely or neatly folded down.

Colors and materials

While you have the uppers side by side, compare the finish and colors of each part and compare the left to the right.

With suede shoes, the leather color may not match from shoe to shoe. For full grain leather shoes, study the emboss pattern to make sure the parts have the same texture. If the leather or mesh parts have a direction to the surface emboss, check that the pattern runs in the same direction.

Stitching

Next, look over the stitching. You are looking for any loose or broken stitches. Be on the lookout for melted stitch ends. The shoe factory will use a heat gun to melt off loose thread ends. This can leave a small fused ball of melted plastic behind.

Double and single needle stitch lines are often mixed on the shoes. Compare the left and right to make sure they match. High quality stitching will be smooth and straight with even spacing. You are looking at the space from the stitch line to the edge of the material and from stitch line to stitch line in the case of a double-needle stitch line.

You should also be on the lookout for empty stitching holes. If a worker over stitches a line, they may try to remove the thread, leaving behind an empty perforation.

Some components may require backstitching or over stitching. You can see on the top eyestay part of the Air Jordan, just to the right of the logo, there is some over stitching. In this case, the eyestay tab is sewn through the lining. The over stitching is where the two touch lines connect. This is not a defect.

Edge treatments

This OG version of the Nike Air Jordan Mid has a special edge treatment not found on the standard Air Jordan Mid. You can see in the photo to the left many of the material edges are rolled. This is a labor-intensive operation as it requires every leather edge to be skived thin then carefully rolled over. The edge rolling operation is a combination of machine and skilled handwork.

Study the shoe to make sure the rolled edges are smooth and constant. The Nike swoosh is die-cut as it's difficult to roll the end edges of tight corners. When inspecting die-cut edges, the key is that they are smooth and clean without any frayed edges. A dull cutting die, or rough cutting mat underneath can cause cut parts to have jagged edges.

Turned edges and collar lines

The top line of the collar line is made by sewing the inner lining to the upper shell, then turning the lining inside the shoe to hide the seam line. The foam padding is glued in place during the folding operation.

This is the most common way to construct a collar top line. A straight stitch line and careful folding of the lining parts will create a smooth collar line.

Look for wrinkles and puckers along the edge. Also, use your fingers to feel for any hard spots caused by over-gluing inside.

Outsoles and midsoles

Study the shoe bottoms. Do they match? Are the color blocks in the same location? Look over the midsole sidewall for wrinkles. Check the seam joining the upper to the outsole. Look for any extra glue on the upper; 2mm is the limit for "over gluing." Look for over buffing of the upper.

On the shoe bottom, check for color bleeding between color blocks. Look for any paint covering mistakes. Check to make sure the outsole parts fit together neatly without any extra glue.

Check that the shoe sits flat on its bottom. Is the sole flat? Check for any soft spots on the bottom of the sole. Soft spots are evidence that the inside of the shoe is not securely glued together.

Examine the top edge of the outsole where it meets the upper. The trimmed edge should be smooth.

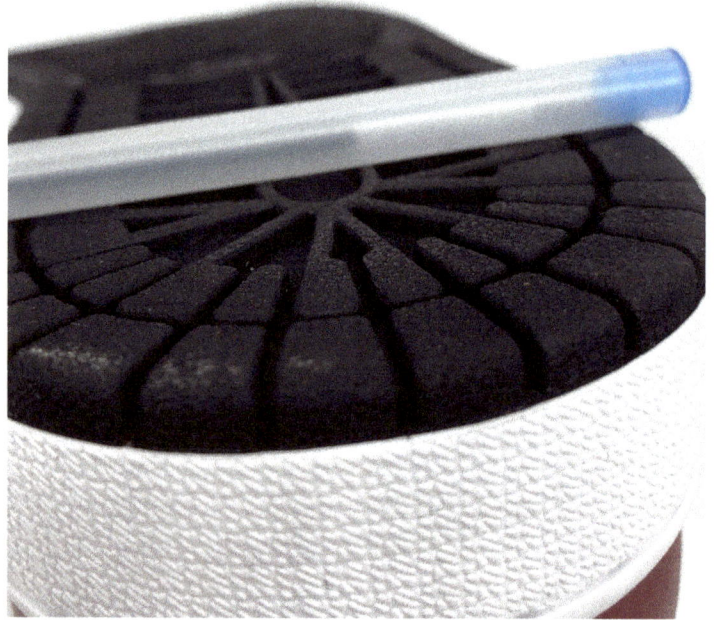

47

Inspect the inside

No inspection is complete without checking the inside of the shoe. Now that we looked over the outside, it's time to dive inside. A great looking shoe with defects inside is not saleable.

First look

Look inside the shoe opening, is the lining clean and free of wrinkles? You should not see any creases, wrinkles, or folds in the heel lining.

Have a look at the footbed. Make sure the footbed is straight, level, and fits correctly. If the footbed is too small it may slide around, too big and the footbed may wrinkle or curl. Folds or creases on the back heel of the footbed are a sure sign of poor shoemaking and will cause the wearer a heel blister.

Next, run your hand down inside. Feel around the edges of the footbed for wrinkles or channel stitching defects.

Check the edges of the tongue for rough stitching or creases in the edges. Make sure to feel where the tongue is attached to the bottom of the shoe's throat. This area can have rough stitching or a hard lump if the foam is not trimmed from the base of the tongue.

Feel all around the collar lining and compare the two shoes to make sure the padding has not shifted inside and does not have any glue spots.

Make sure to reach all the way down into the vamp and toe tip. You are feeling for wrinkles in the front edge of the footbed and any rough stitching.

Feel around for any loose channel stitching threads. These long threads should be trimmed back or secured under the footbed. You can see the tail end of the channel stitching threads are often taped down inside. While not great, this is not a defect.

Under the footbed, you can confirm the shoe is made by the Strobel process.

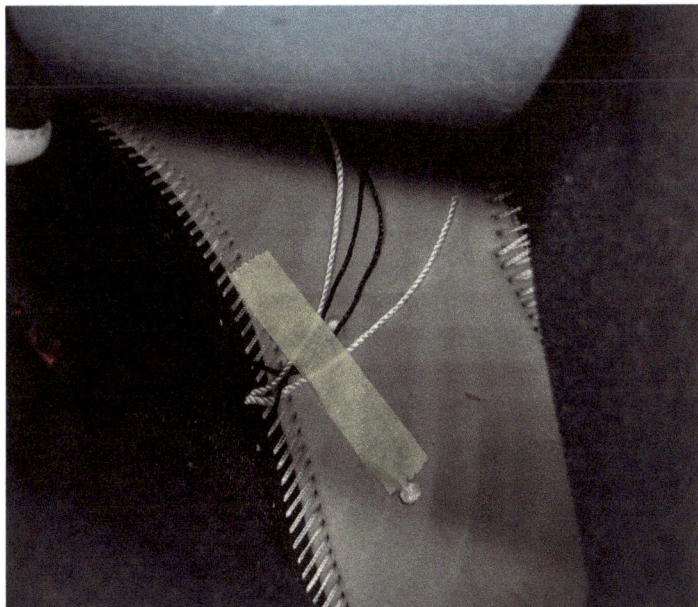

Not perfect

Looking closely, we see some small things that could be better. However, none of these issues stop this shoe from being an A grade.

The foam edge of the eyestay lining can be trimmed back. The melted thread ball can be clipped off. The loose threads along the outsole can be trimmed off.

The red leather dust mixed with glue can be cleaned off the outsole with a rubber eraser.

Even the wavy top line seam can be massaged by hand to smooth it out.

49

Are Air Jordans good shoes?

Yes! Nike makes great shoes. This Air Jordan is a well-made sports shoe. The upper is made with high-quality materials. The workmanship is top grade. The toe and heel counters are properly molded with firm, flexible plastic. The profile is spot on.

Additionally, all outsole parts are clean and carefully trimmed. The color breaks, and mold parting lines are clean. The rubber mold textures are consistent, and the colors are matched correctly.

Assembly wise, the shoe assembly is good. The uppers stand straight, and the outsoles are flat.

Overall, these shoes showcase the high quality and excellent craftsmanship what we expect from Nike.

50

Part 2

Sneaker Product Knowledge

Product knowledge is the backbone of sneaker authentication. Knowing what is "right" is only gained by experience and access to resources. If you are familiar with all the design and construction details of the Nike Air Jordan 1 and know what color materials Nike used, you can easily spot the fakes.

The sneaker market is huge. With so many special colorways, it is a daunting task to know if the shoe you are looking at is something Nike really made. The blue Air Jordan 3 with red accents may be a Footlocker special made for one delivery only in 2018. You may never be able to find a record of that specific version on-line.

You will find that the high-quality photos from sites like StockX and GOAT are incredibly valuable for authentication if you know what to look for.

In this book we have labeled the photos:

Real shoes (R)   and Fake shoes (F)

51

52

Chapter 7 : How to Spot a Fake Nike Air Jordan 1 Mid OG

When Michael Jordan stepped on the court with the Chicago Bulls in 1984, he was wearing what would become known as the Air Jordan 1. The success of Michael Jordan and the Air Jordan led to the introduction of the Air Jordan 2 in 1986. Over the next ten years, Michael Jordan's basketball stardom and Nike's marketing genius propelled the Jordan sneaker franchise to new heights.

To mark the 10th anniversary of the shoe that started it all, Nike relaunched the Air Jordan. The 1994 relaunch was not a success, but it set in motion the re-release concept that would come to dominate the Jordan product range.

Over the next 35 years, the demand for collectible Jordan sneakers grew beyond imagination, creating a brand with sales of over $3 billion a year.

The Air Jordan 1 is THE modern, classic basketball sneaker. The Jordan 1 has joined the Converse All Star and the Adidas Superstar as sneaker legends in the world of sports and fashion.

In the years 2019 and 2020, Nike released over 125 different colors of the Air Jordan 1. Special collaborations with top fashion brands, such as Dior, have driven prices to $30,000 and higher for a single pair of Air Jordan's.

Demand, worldwide popularity, and a steady stream of new models have made the Air Jordan a prime target for sneaker counterfeiters.

Authenticating Air Jordan 1 Mid OG
What to look for

The details
The Air Jordan 1 is not a difficult shoe to build. Die-cut leather parts, a fabric tongue, embossed logos, and two-color rubber cupsole units are easy to acquire. No exotic manufacturing techniques or expensive equipment are required to assemble the Air Jordan 1.

So, how can we authenticate the Jordan 1? If you follow the steps of the authentication checklist and make a proper inspection, you will find the fakes every time. The counterfeiter's greed will always lead to shortcuts and mistakes.

Outsole textures: counterfeiters are in a hurry and never take the time to get the sole texture right. Zoom in on the sidewall and bottom.

Look at every material on the shoe, the fakes are cheap, the material is cheap.

Double or single line stitching: look for smooth, straight, and uniform stitching.

Tongue logo art: did they get the trademark logos correct?

Cut edges should be clean and crisp. Nike demands its equipment be well cared for.

Zoom in on the logos, The art is distinctive.

Are the rolled edges and turned out seam straight and clean? Look for quality workmanship.

Look at the toe and heel. Did the factory use the molding machines to make the correctly shaped toe box and heel counter?

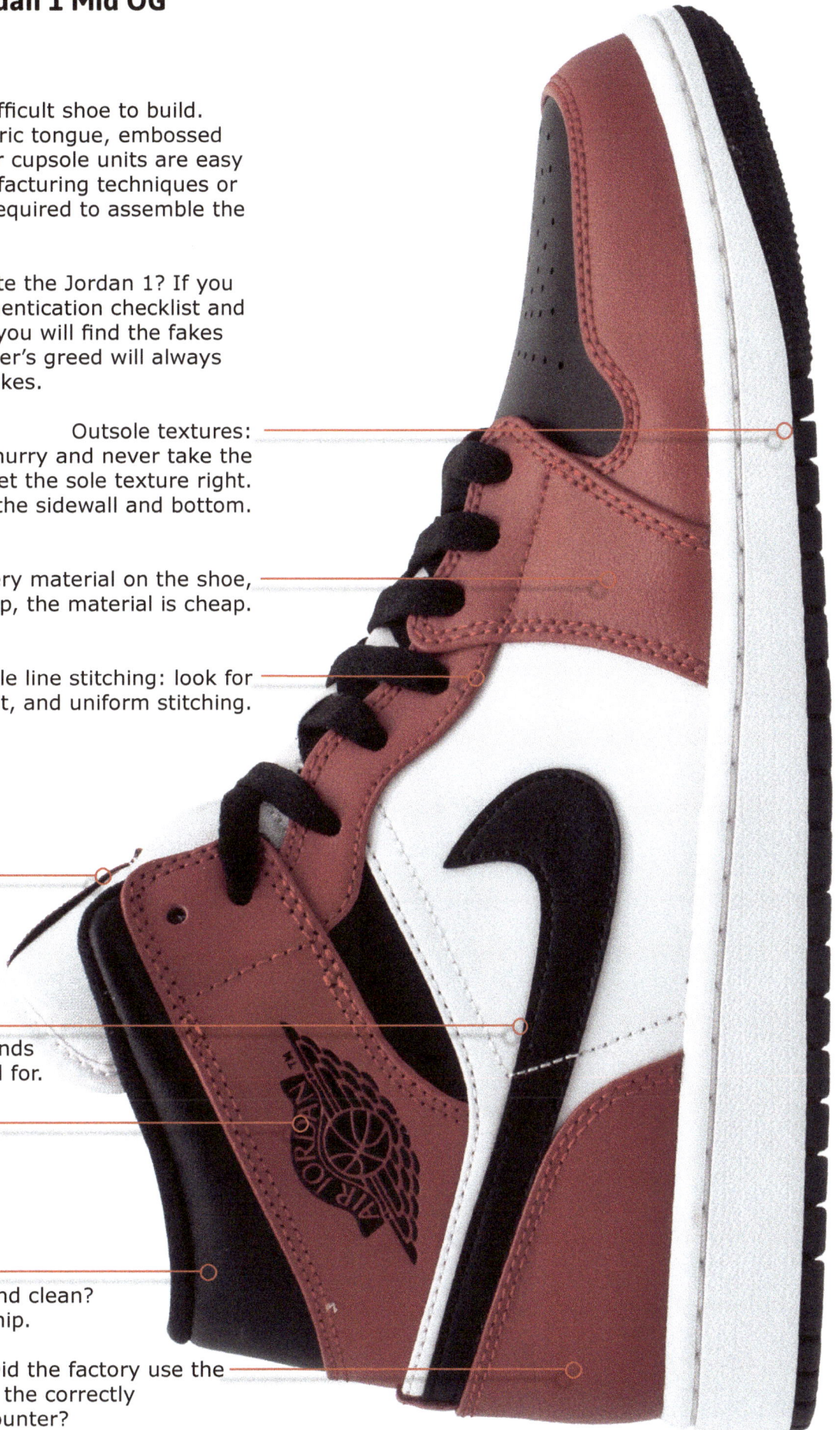

Air Jordan wings logo

Studying the real Air Jordan and the fake Air Jordan side-by-side, you can see the factory making copies did a nice job on the logo.

The artwork on the fake shoe is correct, but the real Jordan 1 logo is embossed a little deeper into the leather.

In this case, it's hard to tell the difference until you look at the pattern of the cut parts. The real Nike does not have any stitching guides to help the stitchers locate the panels during assembly. The red logo panel of the fake Nike is loaded with these little assembly guides.

Assembly guides are not a sign of poor shoe-making, they are very common, but they are not present on the real Air Jordan.

The Jordan 1 heel strap stitching

The Air Jordan 1 has a tiny heel tab that covers the back seams of the quarter panel and the swoosh. You can see the back tab on the real Nike has two stitch lines as the quarter top lines cross over. Also, the black thread contrasts with the grey leather. On the fake Jordan 1, a single black stitch line crosses the black leather tab. The thread color used on the fake matches the leather instead of contrasting with the leather. Again, this detail is not an indication of low-quality shoemaking. It's just not how the original was made.

You can also see the centering guides on the red leather parts of the fake Jordan 1. The centering guides are the small points sticking up from the leather. They aren't inherently bad, but you could consider it a shortcut or sign of lazy construction, and they aren't on the genuine pair of Jordan 1's.

The Jordan 1 tongue logo

Next, get a good look at the woven label attached to the tongue top. The fake Jordan is missing the registered trademark "R." I know it's strange, but Nike likes to have the "R" twice on the woven label.

The Jumpman size tag

For reference, the black tag is the real Nike woven label. Inside the shoe, you will see the size label with the Jordan Jumpman logo. The fake shoe has the tag welded to the back of the tongue. On the real Jordan 1, the tag is sewn down on the inside.

You can also see that the trademark information is in English and French on the true Nike. While the fake has both languages, it has the wrong lettering style, and the tag is stitched on crooked. Crooked parts are a sure sign of poor shoemaking.

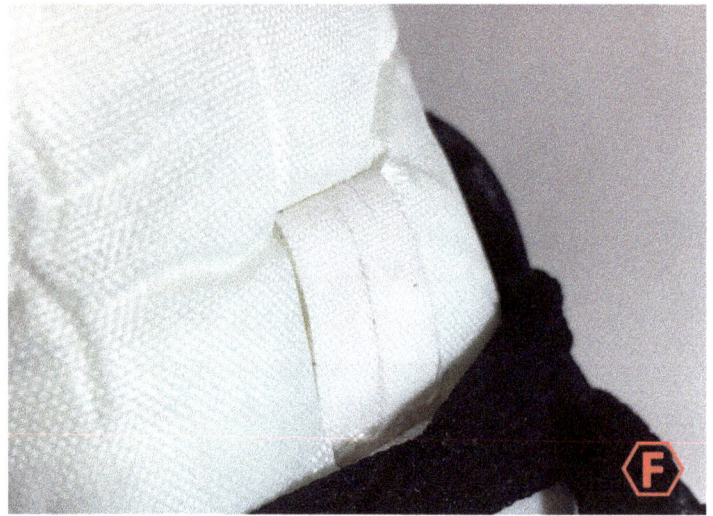

The Jordan 1 tongue lace keeper

The lace keeper is a small point but an obvious tell when looking for fakes. The real Nike shoe has simple cuts in the tongue fabric to act as the lace keeper. This construction looks pretty shoddy for a $120 basketball shoe, but this is how the original was made.

The counterfeit Nike has a small piece of fabric added as the lace keeper.

Jordan 1 quality

Here is an example of a brand that cares for its trademark logo application. You can see the Nike swoosh logo is cleanly die-cut with crisp, clean edges. Nike has selected a quality material with a microfiber backing, and the cutting equipment is in good condition.

The swoosh logo on the counterfeit shoe is a ragged mess. The edge is not cut cleanly, and you can see the fibrous backing of the inexpensive PU leather shredding. This critical branding component must be perfect on a real Nike.

This shredding may be due to a dull cutting die, or the factory has not replaced its cutting mats.

Nike workmanship

This view of the two heels shows how the Nike-made Air Jordan 1 is crafted with more care. The real shoe (to the right) has a smooth top line, and the lining is wrinkle-free as it rolls down into the shoe. The shape of the heel is round and looks like a human foot would fit inside comfortably.

On the left, we see the counterfeit shoe's collar lining is wrinkled, and the overall shape is pinched. The heel counter is not molded with the correct curve, and the lining foam is too soft, allowing the wrinkles to crease the fabric.

The counterfeit factory used cheap sponge foam for the collar padding. They also did not install a heal mold-able heel counter. Instead, they used a solvent-activated heel counter sheet that is pulled into place during the lasting operation instead of a heat press.

The Jordan 1 outsole logo

If you look closely at the Nike logo on the outsole, you can see the fake artwork is wrong. The width of the letters is too narrow. Another obvious mistake is that the "K" of the fake Nike logo is not touching the tail of the swoosh.

Additionally, when you look closely at the tread patterns, you can see the fake red tread has glossy spaces between the tread features where the grey does not.

The outsole parting line

Here we can see the difference between careful rubber outsole pressing with a high-quality mold versus sloppy rubber pressing using substandard equipment. The dividing line between the two rubber colors is called the parting line.

The bottom tread is pressed in the bottom half of the mold, the sidewall in the top side.

The real Air Jordan has a crisp, narrow parting line. The fake outsole has a wide parting line with color bleeding across.

The midsole

This is an interesting discovery. Inside the forefoot we see the fake has something extra! Usually there is something missing inside a fake shoe. In this case, the fake has an EVA midsole that does NOT belong.

The real Air Jordan 1 has a PU wedge midsole that ends just behind the ball of the foot. Our fake shoe has an inexpensive die-cut EVA slab.

The missing air bag

This is more typical of what you will see inside a fake shoe...nothing! Our authentic shoe has the correct HF welded airbag encased in poured PU foam.

The counterfeiters skipped the expensive hidden airbag and installed a full-length EVA sheet as seen in the photo above.

60

Authentic Air Jordan 1 Mid OG

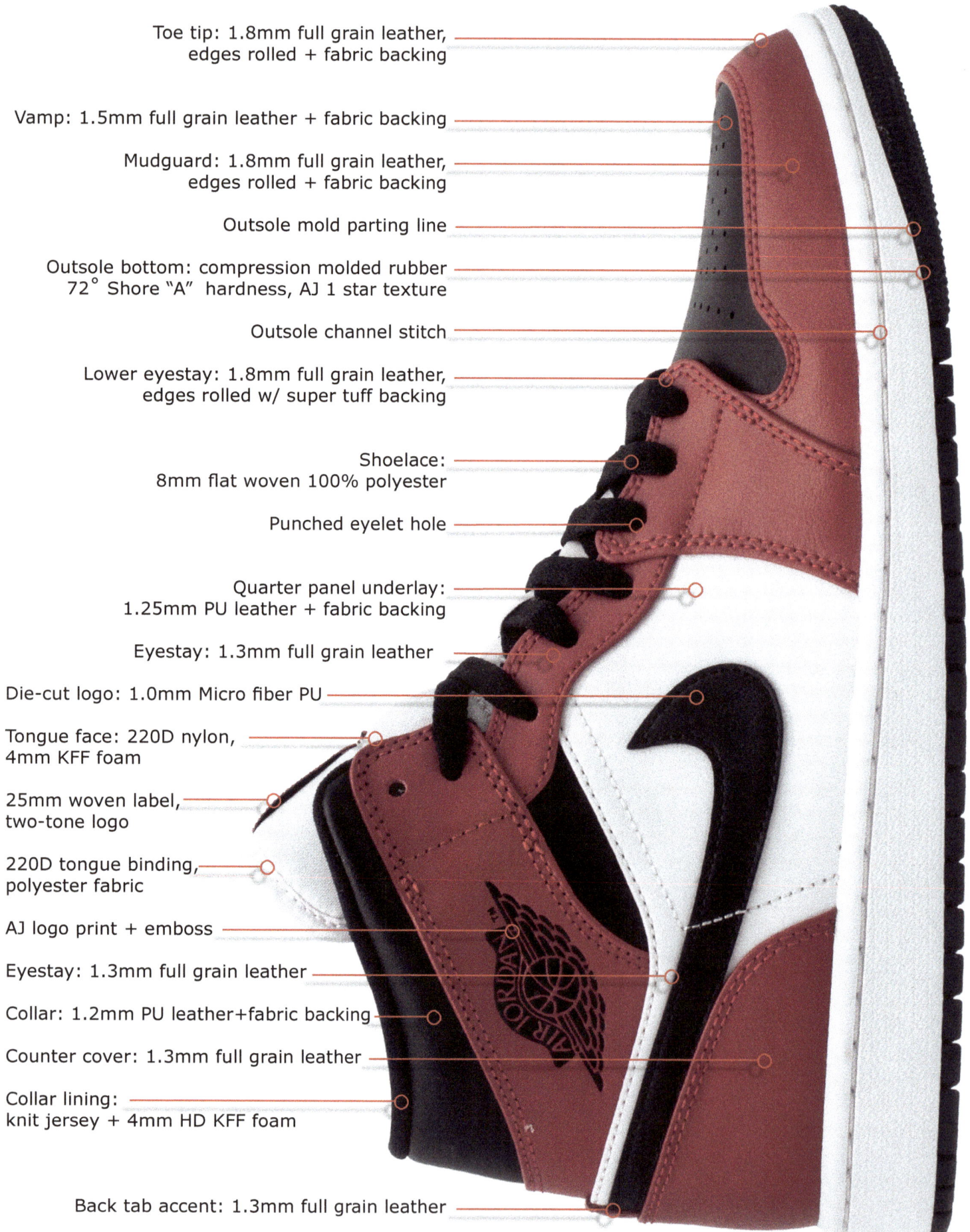

Toe tip: 1.8mm full grain leather, edges rolled + fabric backing

Vamp: 1.5mm full grain leather + fabric backing

Mudguard: 1.8mm full grain leather, edges rolled + fabric backing

Outsole mold parting line

Outsole bottom: compression molded rubber 72° Shore "A" hardness, AJ 1 star texture

Outsole channel stitch

Lower eyestay: 1.8mm full grain leather, edges rolled w/ super tuff backing

Shoelace: 8mm flat woven 100% polyester

Punched eyelet hole

Quarter panel underlay: 1.25mm PU leather + fabric backing

Eyestay: 1.3mm full grain leather

Die-cut logo: 1.0mm Micro fiber PU

Tongue face: 220D nylon, 4mm KFF foam

25mm woven label, two-tone logo

220D tongue binding, polyester fabric

AJ logo print + emboss

Eyestay: 1.3mm full grain leather

Collar: 1.2mm PU leather+fabric backing

Counter cover: 1.3mm full grain leather

Collar lining: knit jersey + 4mm HD KFF foam

Back tab accent: 1.3mm full grain leather

61

Fake Air Jordan 1

Toe tip profile: wrong, it is laid back

Edge not rolled

Rough cutting edge

Parting line shows color bleeding

Rough stitching + over stitch

Incorrect sidewall rubber texture

Rough stitching and cutting and wrong material

Tongue face: notice foam yellowing

Incorrect swoosh logo

Rough cutting

Alignment nibs showing

Wavy rolled seam

Wrong collar material

Alignment nibs showing

F

Authentic Air Jordan 1 Mid OG

Toe tip: 1.8mm full grain leather, edges rolled + fabric backing

Vamp: 1.5mm full grain leather, perforated + fabric backing

No forefoot midsole: Yes, this is correct

Vamp lining: smooth jersey mesh 2mm high density PU foam, tricot backing

One piece tongue & vamp lining covers toe tip stitching and joined to quarter lining with flat lock stitch

200gsm stitched bonded polyester

Tongue face: 220D nylon, 2mm KFF PU foam, tricot backing

Tongue lining: smooth jersey mesh, 2mm high density PU foam, tricot backing

Tongue binding: 15mm 220D nylon tape, double rolled edges with 5mm exposure

Quarter backing/lining: 100% polyester, low stretch, square weave fabric

Size mark heat transfer logo

25mm woven label: two-tone logo label

Poured PU foam midsole wedge Asker "C" 45°

RF welded .5mm TPU film 5 column air cell with PU foam over mold

Compression molded rubber 72° Shore "A" hardness

Sockliner cover: 100% polyester brushed Nylex

Die-cut 5mm PU foam sheet Durometer Asker "C" 25°

Collar lining: smooth jersey mesh +2mm HD KFF PU foam backing

15mm KFF PU foam, tricot backing

Heel counter: 2.5mm Surlyn sheet, heat molded

®

Inside the Fake Air Jordan 1

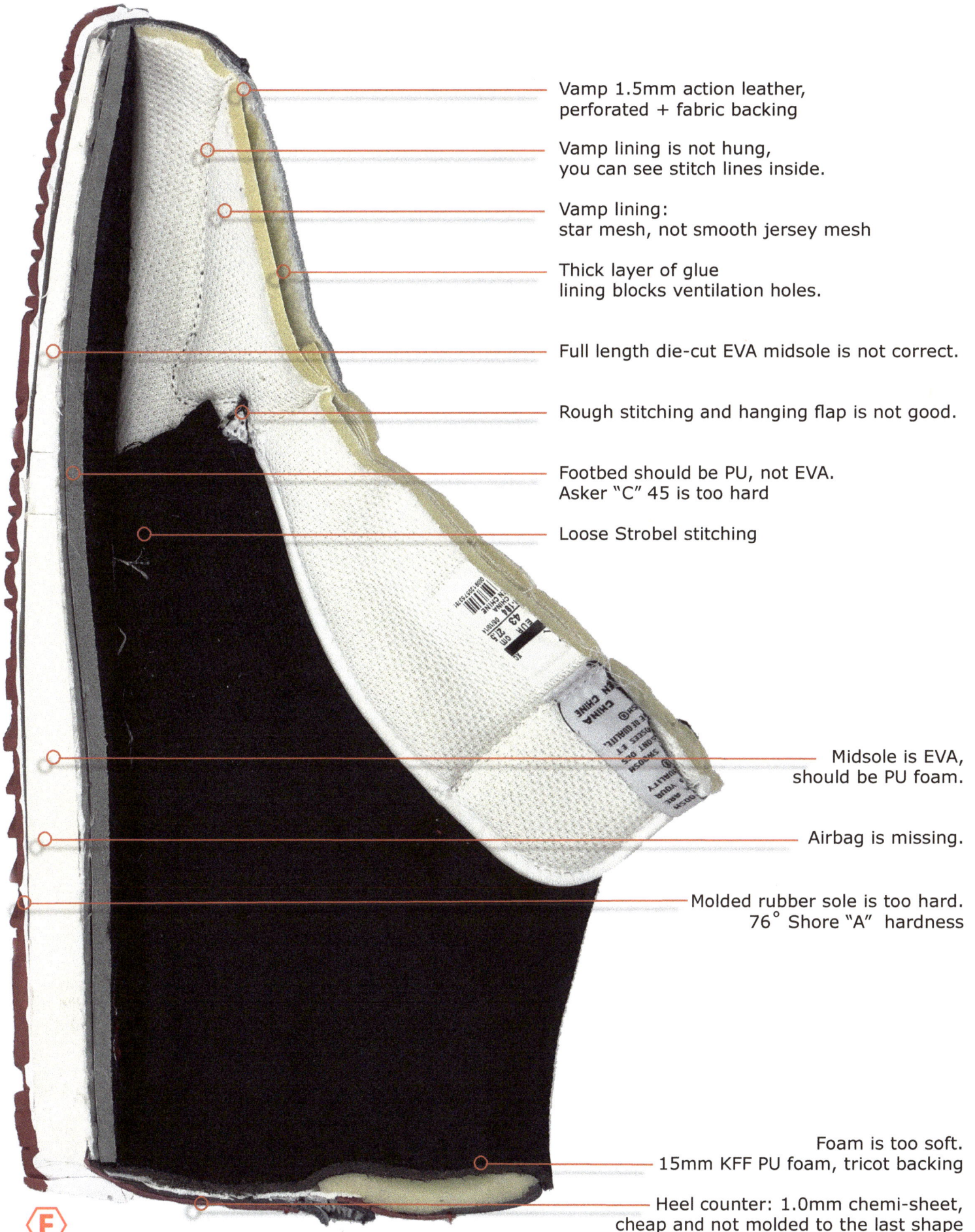

Vamp 1.5mm action leather, perforated + fabric backing

Vamp lining is not hung, you can see stitch lines inside.

Vamp lining: star mesh, not smooth jersey mesh

Thick layer of glue lining blocks ventilation holes.

Full length die-cut EVA midsole is not correct.

Rough stitching and hanging flap is not good.

Footbed should be PU, not EVA. Asker "C" 45 is too hard

Loose Strobel stitching

Midsole is EVA, should be PU foam.

Airbag is missing.

Molded rubber sole is too hard. 76° Shore "A" hardness

Foam is too soft. 15mm KFF PU foam, tricot backing

Heel counter: 1.0mm chemi-sheet, cheap and not molded to the last shape

F

Chapter 8 : How to Spot a Fake Nike ZoomX Vaporfly NEXT %

The ZoomX Vaporfly NEXT% was destined to be a target for counterfeiting operations from the day of its launch. Its high price and trendsetting performance/fashion design made it instantly popular with athletes, celebrities, posers, and collectors. The ZoomX foam look is also relatively easy to copy. Its advances in material and cushioning technology are hidden from the outside, so the manufacturing of the counterfeit from an outside perspective is not difficult.

The ZoomX Vaporfly NEXT% is an interesting case for study due to its simple construction. What makes the authentic shoe so special is not random accessories; it's the high-performance materials Nike used. To the untrained eye, it's not easy to see exactly what's wrong with counterfeit versions of the shoe, but if you follow the authentication checklist, it will be obvious.

Authenticating ZoomX Vaporfly NEXT%
What to look for:

Materials

Counterfeiters can not afford to use the same high-tech materials that Nike builds into the ZoomX. The authentication should start with the midsole flex test. The most expensive part of the ZoomX is the hidden carbon plate and because the plate cannot be seen from the outside of the shoe, it will be left off.

The real Nike ZoomX has a single color semi-translucent paint fade, not two colors.

Look for the 3D RF welding effect on the eyestay parts.

Look closely at the Vaporweave fabric.

The real ZoomX has a Pebax foam midsole, the surface will be finely wrinkled.

Look at the cut pattern part, easy to overlook but a significant sign the shoe is real.

Feel for the cement bonding line that joins the upper and lower midsoles

Provenance

The two sample shoes we have are both of known origin. The authentic Nike-made pair came from a friend who purchased them from Nike online and raced in them, compressing the midsole in the process. While this pair did arrive used without its box, we know the source, confirming it's real. The counterfeit pair was purchased from Aliexpress.com and delivered from China. Interestingly, the inner label of the shoe claims the shoe was manufactured in Vietnam. This is possible, but the real Nike shoe is "Made in China." Our mail-order shoe arrived without a box which is an instant red flag.

We also tried to scan the inner label barcode, which was unsuccessful with the counterfeit shoe. You can see the tongue labels are very different, so if you know what the authentic label looks like, you can very easily spot a fake.

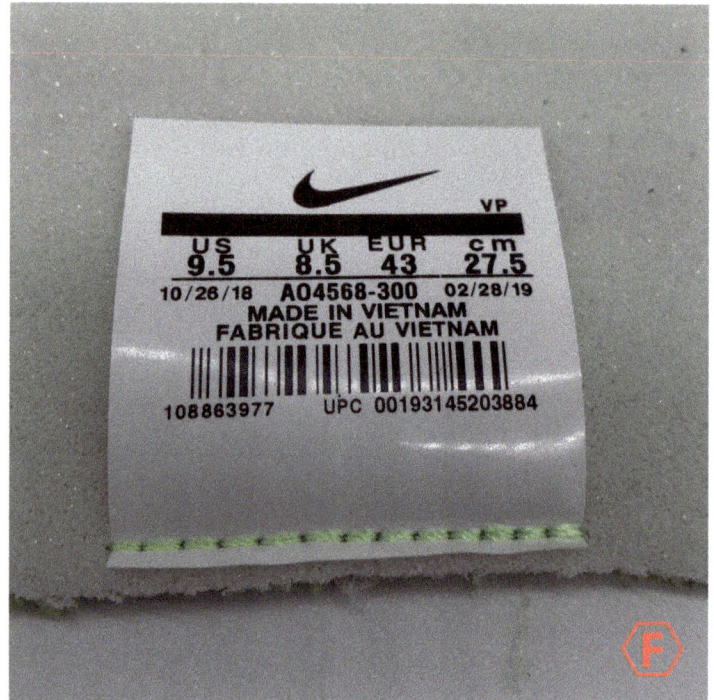

Quality inspection

The ZoomX does present an interesting challenge in the case of a quality check. The upper design and construction of the authentic shoe looks a bit rough and wrinkled due to the raw, die-cut edges and exposed flatlock stitching. To authenticate this shoe, we will need to look past these issues and study the shoe closely.

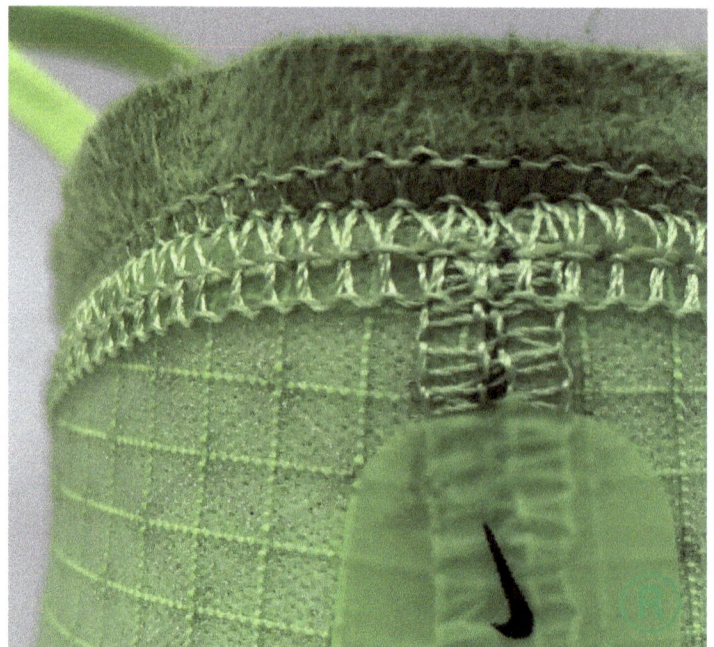

Color matching

The color match of the counterfeit shoe is a problem. The flatlock stitching thread around the top line is too bright.

The midsole paint fade is not color correct either. The real ZoomX has a semi-translucent paint spray that makes the fade effect with one color pass. The fake shoe uses yellow and green paint to replicate the effect.

Finally, the side swoosh should be black, but on the fake, the logo is gray.

Heel View

As we follow the standard inspection procedure, we can see the heel of the real shoe is straight up and down with the Vapormesh cemented flat to the heel counter surface.

Here we can see the counterfeit heel is a bit wrinkled, with the logo warped and off-center. Also, the topline is crooked, and the material color is different.

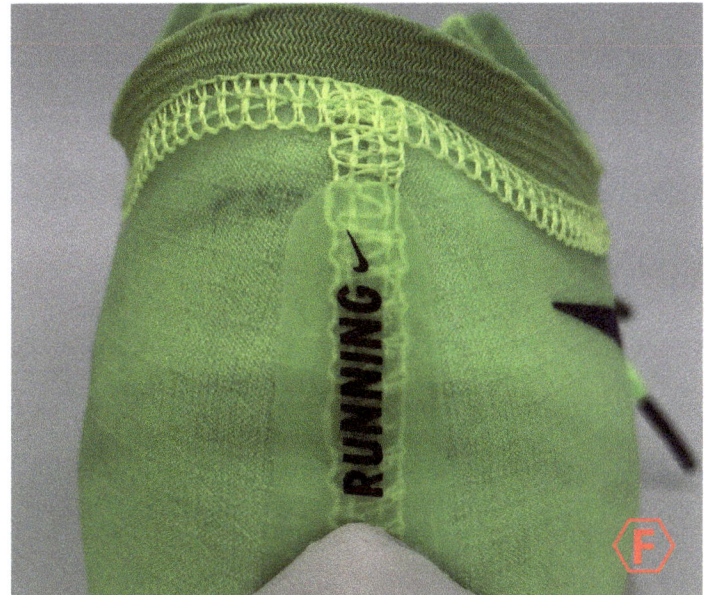

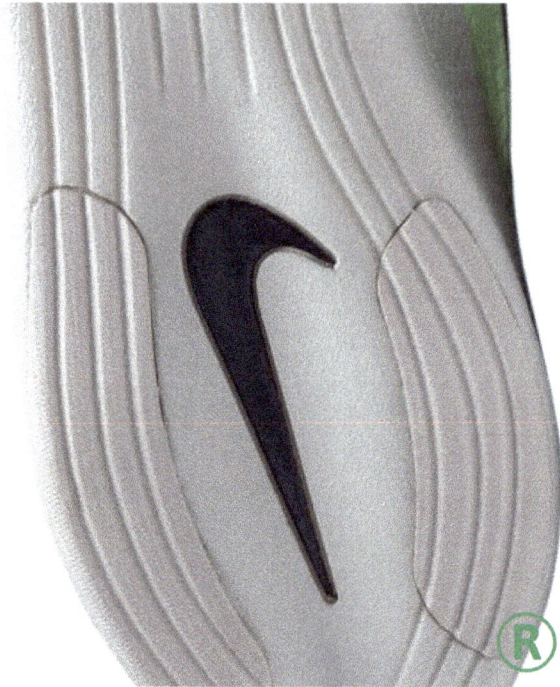

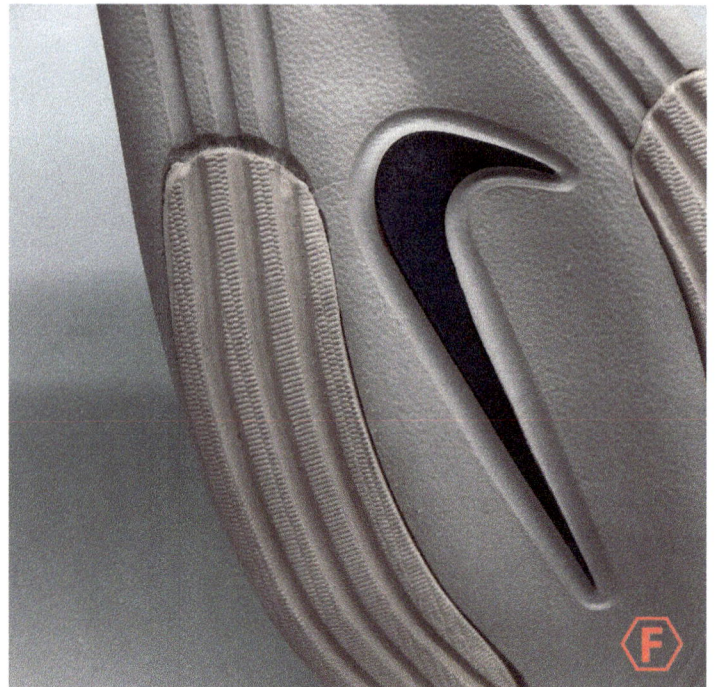

Bottom

When we inspect the bottom, we can see the rubber parts of the real shoe fit together neatly with uniform edge gaps. This is what proper stocking fitting with high quality, and high tolerance parts look like. The counterfeit shoe has some stock fitting problems. The heel pod doesn't fit snugly into the midsole; you can see glue in the gaps. This part on the authentic shoe is perfect, with the parts fitting tight together.

Finally, on the bottom of the outsole, you can see the swoosh on the fake shoe has a wider color dam molded into the EVA foam.

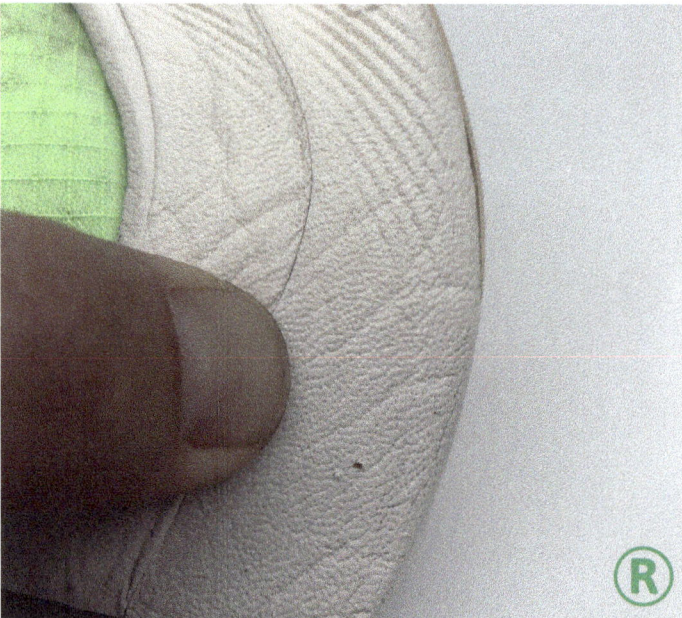

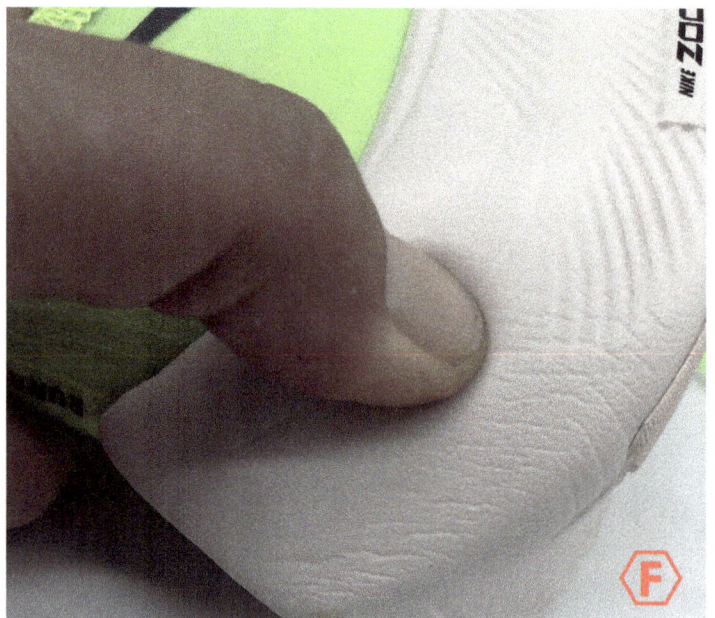

Midsole construction

The Nike ZoomX is a conventionally assembled shoe. The Strobel upper is attached by cold cement process to the outsole unit. Both the real and counterfeit shoes are made this way.

It's the design and construction of the authentic shoe's outsole unit that is so special. The real ZoomX is made from two layers of Pebax foam with a full-length carbon fiber spring shank inside.

You can't see the shank without cutting the shoe (we will get to that later), but you can easily feel the edge where the two halves of the midsole are bonded together. The glued surfaces make a hard ridge in the foam, you can't see it, but you can feel it.

You can see and feel on the counterfeit shoe that there is no bonding ridge.

69

Carbon plate

A simple flex test will also show you there is no carbon shank in the copy shoe. The fake shoe can be folded. The authentic shoe is very difficult to bend.

The energy return of the carbon is a key performance feature of the ZoomX.

Midsole foam

While we are looking at the midsole, we should take note of the midsole foam materials. Study the surface of the foam carefully. You will see the authentic midsole has a very finely detailed surface texture. This highly detailed surface is due to the midsole being compression molded. Compression molding allows more defined surface textures and more dimensionally stable parts.

This is why the fake shoe has gaps around the rubber pods. The fake is made by the injection EVA forming process.

When you see inside the cross-section of the counterfeit, it will be obvious.
Note for this photo; the fake shoe is on the right, the real shoe is on the left.

70

Vaporfly mesh upper

We have seen the heart of the ZoomX Vapor-fly NEXT% is its advanced materials. The carbon spring shank and Pebax foam midsole are not the only special components. The authentic shoe's upper mesh and microfiber suede parts are very different from the knock-off copy.

The Nike Vaporweave upper mesh on the authentic shoe has a strong vertical and horizontal component, while the 45° fiber component of the weave is slightly lighter.

The 45° fiber component of the counterfeit weave has a darker appearance. Also, notice the underlying pattern of the fake is sharper in the corner.

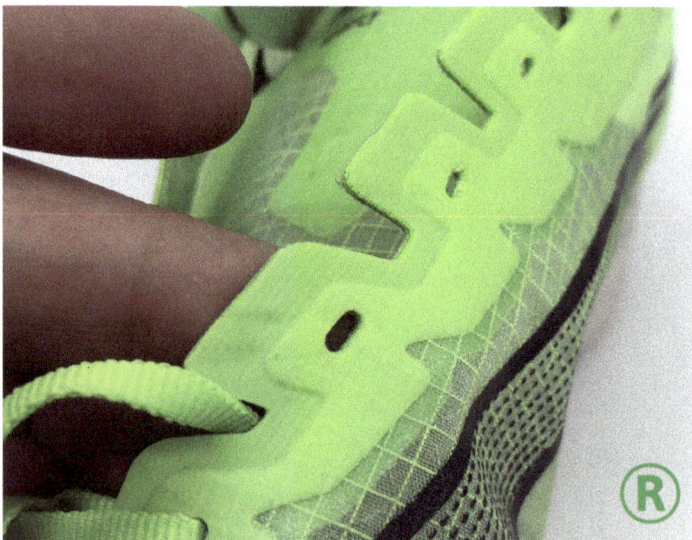

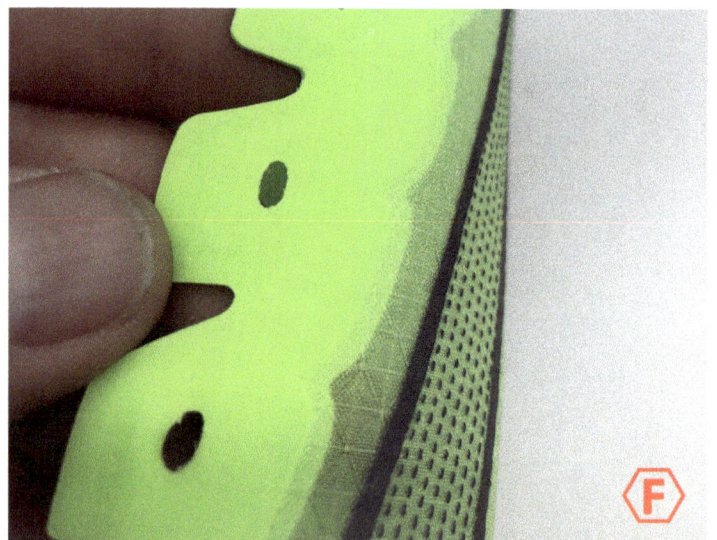

Eyestay

The RF welded TPP eyestay overlay covers a thin layer of super tough reinforcement. The welding operation is done with a 3D mold. In the authentic Nike, you can see the step-up of the reinforcement part.

The copy shoe has some reinforcements but is welded with a flat tool.

Tongue and collar

The tongue face and top collar of the ZoomX are made with the same green microfiber suede material. If you look closely, you will see the real shoe has a suede backing, while the counterfeit Nike has a knit fabric backing.

Take a quick look at the tongue; on the real shoe, the welding and microfiber are the same shade of green. Not so on the counterfeit.

These are exactly the flaws a quick review of photos online will reveal to you.

Look at the pattern parts for the Microfiber, TPU weld, and Vapormesh. On the real ZoomX tongue, the cut edges match up. On the fake tongue (on the right), you can see the edges of the weld don't follow the edge of the microfiber. The lighter green is the misaligned TPU weld.

Heel counter

The heel counter of the counterfeit shoe is much thinner than the real shoe. If you give the fake shoe the heel squeeze test, it will bend and buckle. The authentic Nike heel counter is thicker and molded into shape. It will not buckle.

The collar foam padding on the fake shoe is less than half the thickness of the collar foam padding on the authentic shoe. The real shoe is shown on the right side in each of these photos.

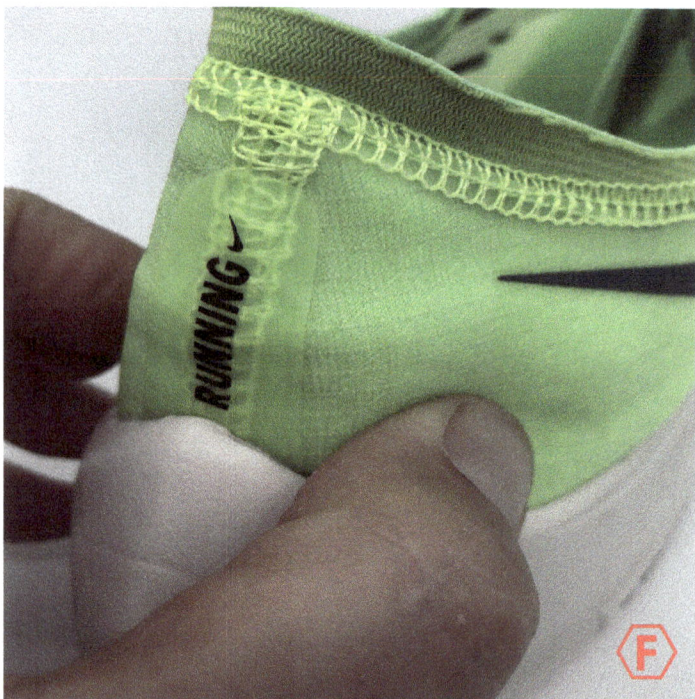

Shoe inside

Inside the shoe, we can see that Nike has glued the footbed down. The glue stripes are from the cementing machine. Inside the fake shoe, the footbed is free-floating.

While we are looking at the footbeds, we can see the Nike has a thicker footbed made of EVA foam. The flat solid color and invisible cell structure tell you this is EVA foam. The slightly sparkling surface and visible cell structure on the fake shoe is a sign this footbed is made from crystallized PU foam.

Amazingly, you can see through the footbed of the fake shoe. You can see the outline of the footbed logo. This footbed will provide comfort for just a few days before it is compacted flat.

Under the footbed, you can see the authentic Nike has the size mark printed on the Strobel. The real Nike Strobel has a longitudinal weave and thicker foam padding.

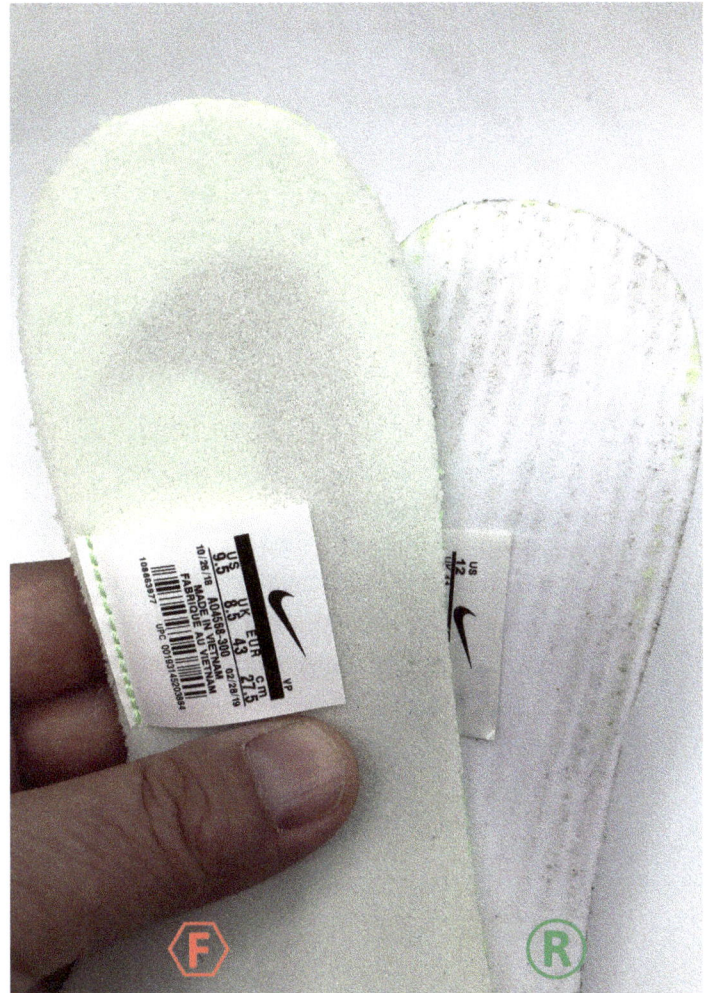

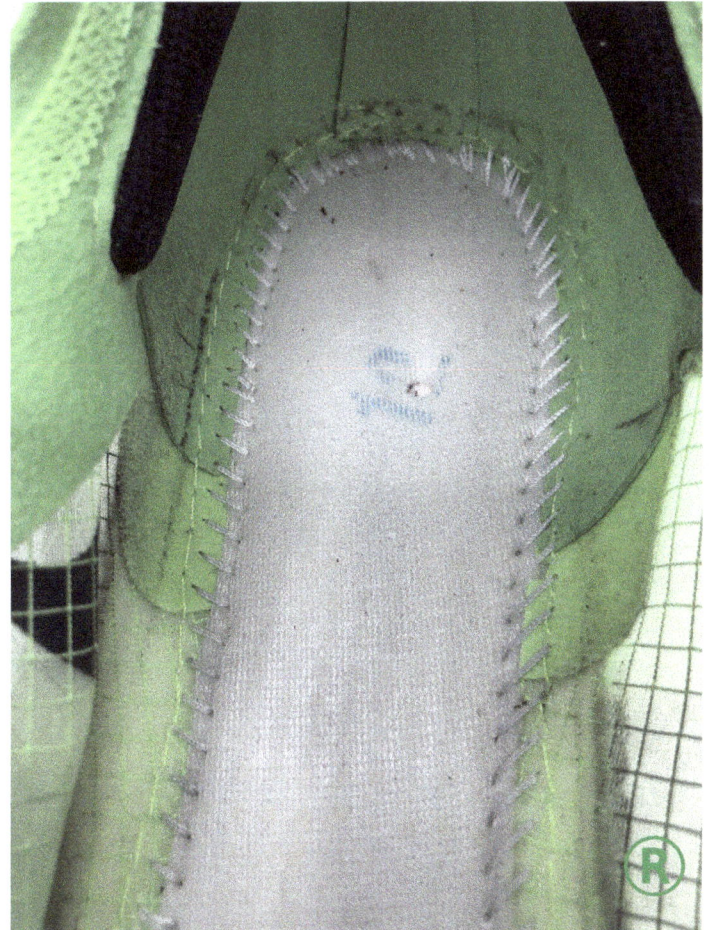

Authentic Nike ZoomX

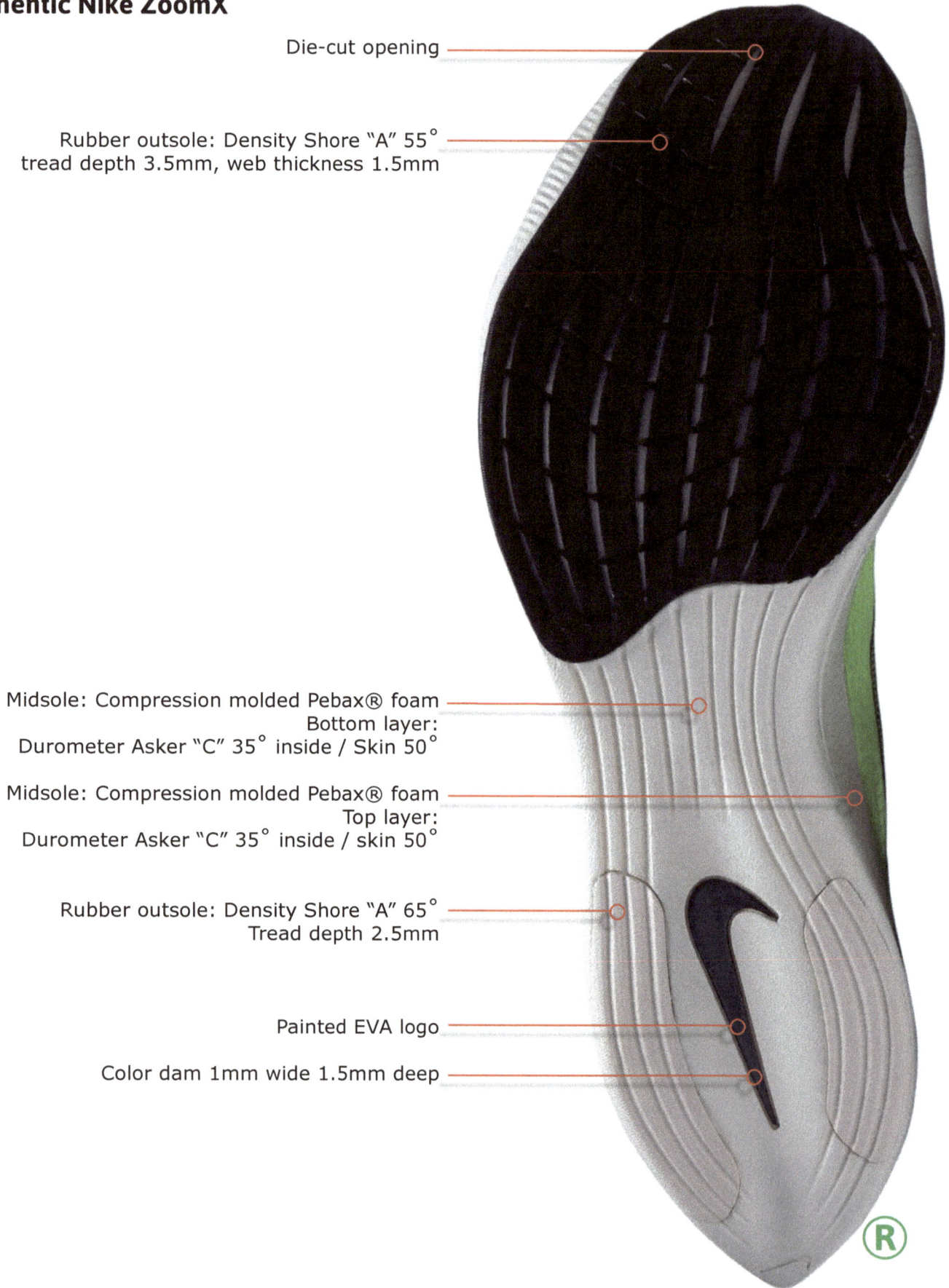

Die-cut opening

Rubber outsole: Density Shore "A" 55°
tread depth 3.5mm, web thickness 1.5mm

Midsole: Compression molded Pebax® foam
Bottom layer:
Durometer Asker "C" 35° inside / Skin 50°

Midsole: Compression molded Pebax® foam
Top layer:
Durometer Asker "C" 35° inside / skin 50°

Rubber outsole: Density Shore "A" 65°
Tread depth 2.5mm

Painted EVA logo

Color dam 1mm wide 1.5mm deep

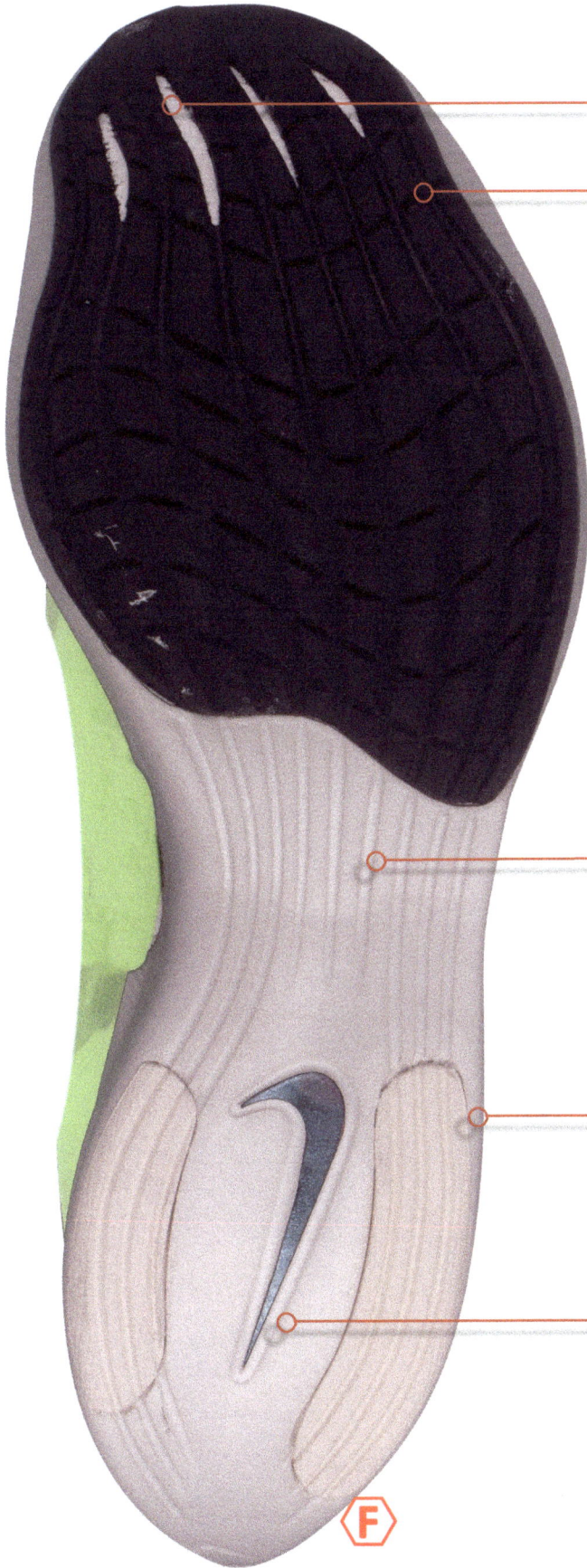

Die-cut openings are ragged, poor trimming.

Rubber outsole: Density Shore "A" 65°, tread depth 3.5mm, web thickness 1.5mm
The rubber is harder and heavier than the real Nike compound.

Injection molded EVA foam midsole
Durometer Asker "C" 40° inside / skin 55°
Single layer is the wrong compound and is missing the carbon shank.

Rubber outsole: Density Shore "A" 65°
Tread depth 2.5mm

Color dam is 1.5mm wide
Much wider than the real ZoomX.

F

Authentic Nike ZoomX

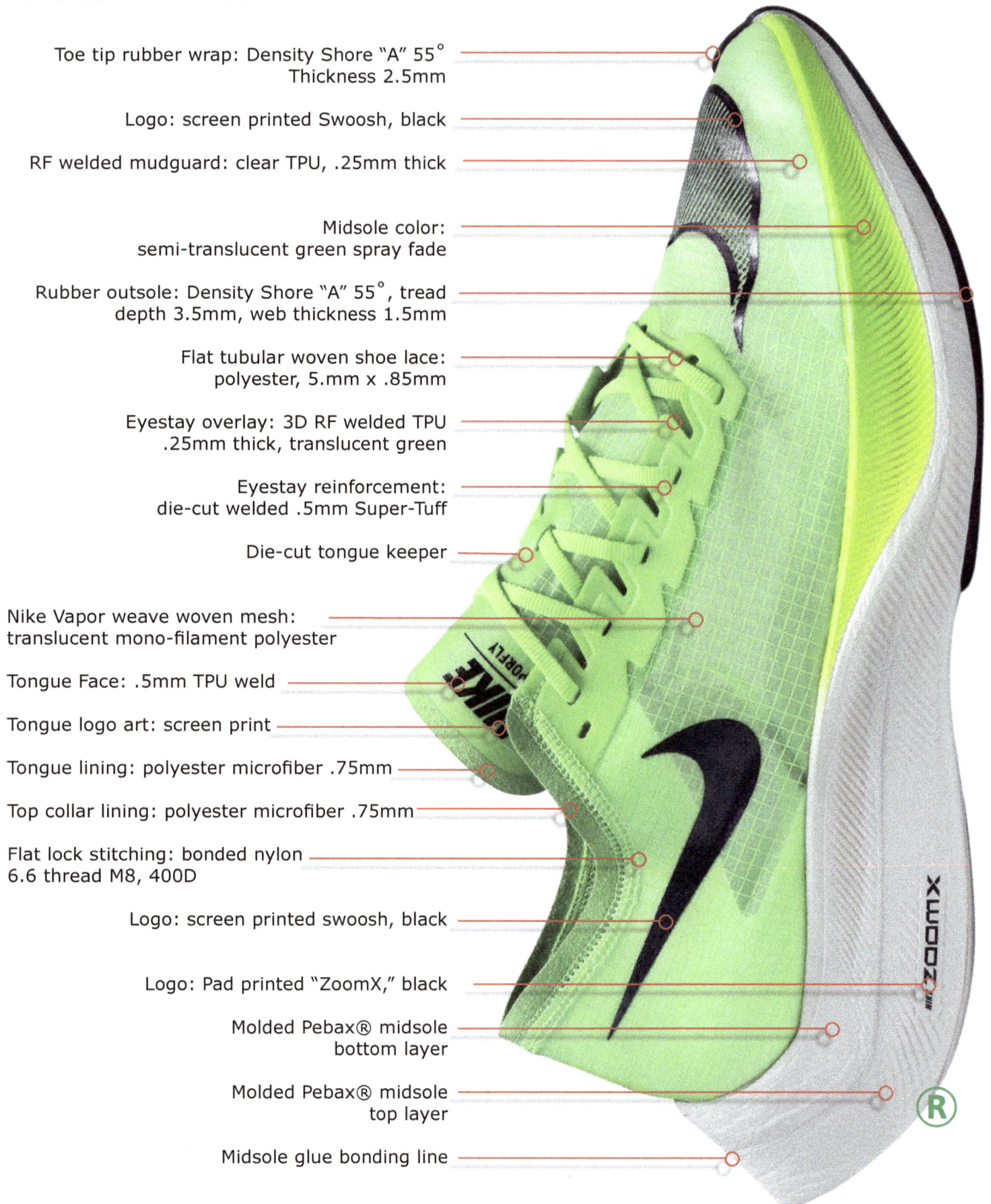

Toe tip rubber wrap: Density Shore "A" 55°
Thickness 2.5mm

Logo: screen printed Swoosh, black

RF welded mudguard: clear TPU, .25mm thick

Midsole color:
semi-translucent green spray fade

Rubber outsole: Density Shore "A" 55°, tread
depth 3.5mm, web thickness 1.5mm

Flat tubular woven shoe lace:
polyester, 5.mm x .85mm

Eyestay overlay: 3D RF welded TPU
.25mm thick, translucent green

Eyestay reinforcement:
die-cut welded .5mm Super-Tuff

Die-cut tongue keeper

Nike Vapor weave woven mesh:
translucent mono-filament polyester

Tongue Face: .5mm TPU weld

Tongue logo art: screen print

Tongue lining: polyester microfiber .75mm

Top collar lining: polyester microfiber .75mm

Flat lock stitching: bonded nylon
6.6 thread M8, 400D

Logo: screen printed swoosh, black

Logo: Pad printed "ZoomX," black

Molded Pebax® midsole
bottom layer

Molded Pebax® midsole
top layer

Midsole glue bonding line

Fake Nike ZoomX

Toe tip rubber: The rubber is harder and heavier than the real Nike compound

Swoosh logo: not the correct color

Midsole color: is two color opaque spray. Not correct.

Rubber outsole: Density Shore "A" 65° tread depth 3.5mm, web thickness 1.5mm
The rubber is harder and heavier than the real Nike compound.

Flat tubular woven shoe lace: polyester 5.mm x .85mm. Aglet color is wrong

Eyestay reinforcement: die-cut welded .5mm Super-Tuff. Eyestay weld is flat missing 3D effect

Nike Vaporweave copy mesh is not correct.

Polyester microfiber .6mm is too thin and has incorrect backing

Flat lock stitching: not color matched

Polyester microfiber .6mm is too thin and has incorrect backing

Counter lining underlay pattern is incorrect

Logo: swoosh color is wrong

Midsole: incorrect Pebax® foam

Polyester microfiber .6mm is too thin and has incorrect backing

Heel counter: cover fabric is wrinkled

Midsole: bonding line is missing, the fake midsole is only one piece, and the carbon shank is missing.

F

Authentic Nike ZoomX

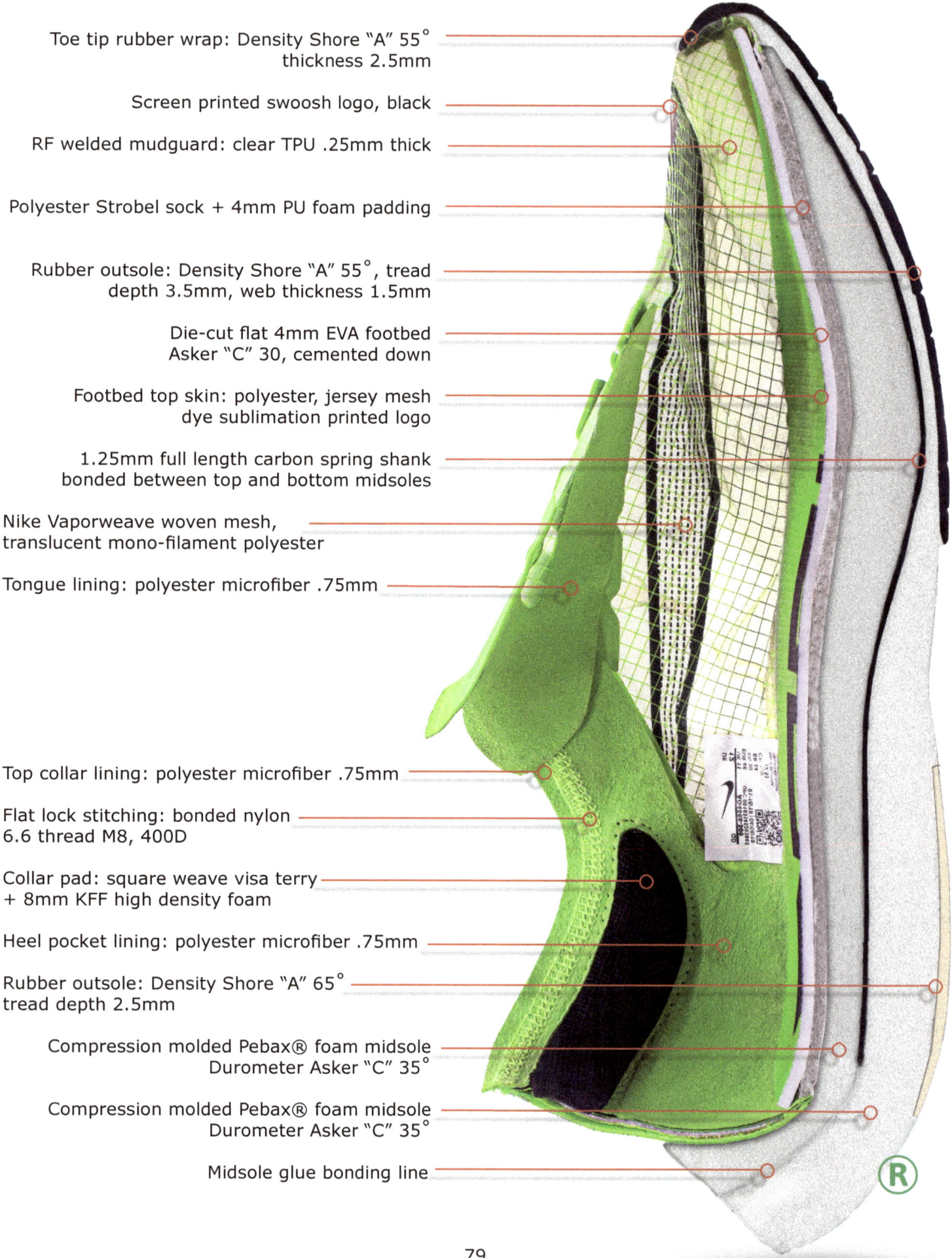

Toe tip rubber wrap: Density Shore "A" 55°
thickness 2.5mm

Screen printed swoosh logo, black

RF welded mudguard: clear TPU .25mm thick

Polyester Strobel sock + 4mm PU foam padding

Rubber outsole: Density Shore "A" 55°, tread
depth 3.5mm, web thickness 1.5mm

Die-cut flat 4mm EVA footbed
Asker "C" 30, cemented down

Footbed top skin: polyester, jersey mesh
dye sublimation printed logo

1.25mm full length carbon spring shank
bonded between top and bottom midsoles

Nike Vaporweave woven mesh,
translucent mono-filament polyester

Tongue lining: polyester microfiber .75mm

Top collar lining: polyester microfiber .75mm

Flat lock stitching: bonded nylon
6.6 thread M8, 400D

Collar pad: square weave visa terry
+ 8mm KFF high density foam

Heel pocket lining: polyester microfiber .75mm

Rubber outsole: Density Shore "A" 65°
tread depth 2.5mm

Compression molded Pebax® foam midsole
Durometer Asker "C" 35°

Compression molded Pebax® foam midsole
Durometer Asker "C" 35°

Midsole glue bonding line

Fake Nike ZOOMx

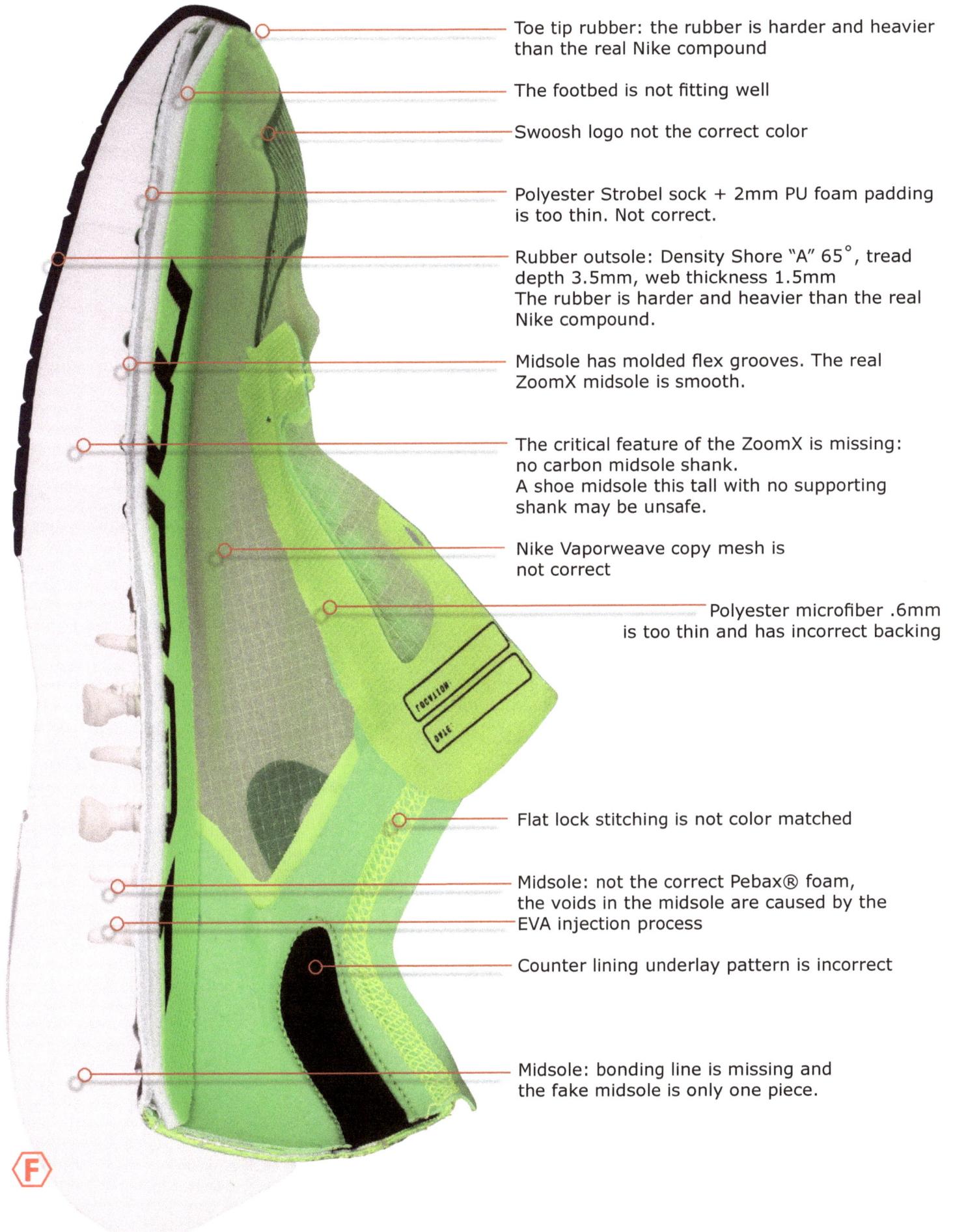

Toe tip rubber: the rubber is harder and heavier than the real Nike compound

The footbed is not fitting well

Swoosh logo not the correct color

Polyester Strobel sock + 2mm PU foam padding is too thin. Not correct.

Rubber outsole: Density Shore "A" 65°, tread depth 3.5mm, web thickness 1.5mm
The rubber is harder and heavier than the real Nike compound.

Midsole has molded flex grooves. The real ZoomX midsole is smooth.

The critical feature of the ZoomX is missing: no carbon midsole shank.
A shoe midsole this tall with no supporting shank may be unsafe.

Nike Vaporweave copy mesh is not correct

Polyester microfiber .6mm is too thin and has incorrect backing

Flat lock stitching is not color matched

Midsole: not the correct Pebax® foam, the voids in the midsole are caused by the EVA injection process

Counter lining underlay pattern is incorrect

Midsole: bonding line is missing and the fake midsole is only one piece.

F

Chapter 9 : How to Spot a Fake Vans Old Skool

The Vans Old Skool is a classic sneaker that also happens to be an "evergreen" style. An evergreen style is a wardrobe basic that sells year after year and makes Vans green money year after year. The Old Skool's evergreen status makes it a prime target for counterfeit production.

The upper design is easy to manufacture, the suede and canvas materials that make up the shoe upper are common. The Old Skool should be an easy shoe to copy, right? Wrong. The Vans Old Skool is made using the classic (some would say a technically obsolete) method of manufacturing; vulcanization.

In chapter 3, we reviewed the difference between vulcanized and cold cement shoes. What we did not discuss was the equipment required to make vulcanized shoes.

A vulcanizing factory requires all the standard upper making equipment AND the equipment to mix and shape the rubber parts. The rubber mixing machines and vulcanizing ovens are expensive to buy and operate. The counterfeiting operations would much rather buy the molded rubber outsole units complete on the open market and quickly slap together the upper. You will see in the next few pages why this is important to authenticating Vans shoes. Cold cement footwear production is by far the most common method of sneaker manufacturing. Cold cement construction is fast, efficient, and economical and does not require expensive rubber mixing equipment.

81

Authenticating Vans Old Skool
What to look for

Construction

Many counterfeiters will skip trying to make the shoe with the authentic vulcanized process. Look closely at the sole. The authentic Old Skool sole has bulges, ripples, and waves. The sole is made of three layers of foxing tape.

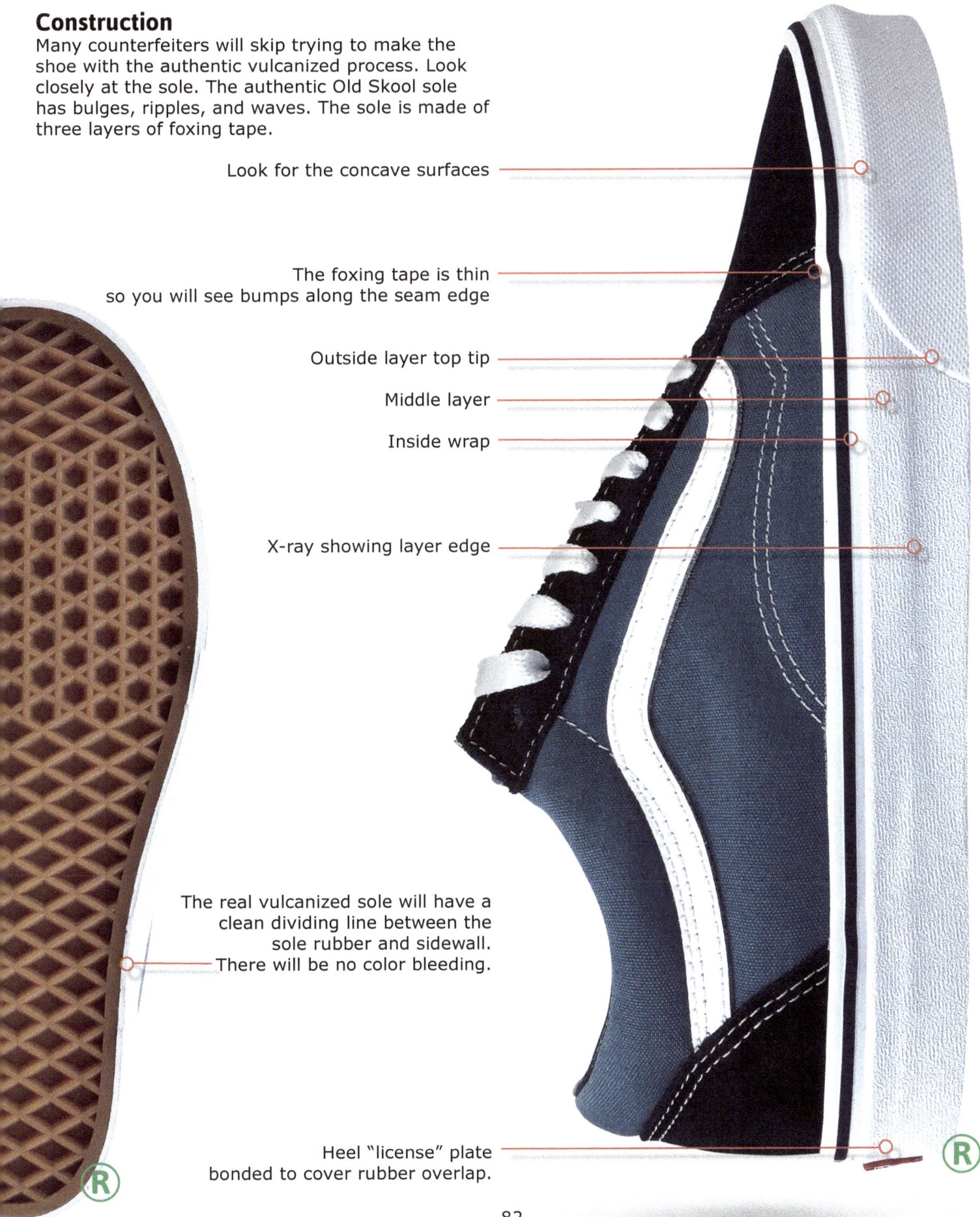

Look for the concave surfaces

The foxing tape is thin so you will see bumps along the seam edge

Outside layer top tip

Middle layer

Inside wrap

X-ray showing layer edge

The real vulcanized sole will have a clean dividing line between the sole rubber and sidewall. There will be no color bleeding.

Heel "license" plate bonded to cover rubber overlap.

®

®

82

Is the Vans sole stripe real or fake?

The first thing to look at is the sole stripe. The stripe on the rubber foxing tape is a trademark styling cue for the Vans classic. When studying the colored stripe ranging across the whole shoe, notice that the rubber stripe is color molded. It is solid colored rubber, meaning the edges will be clean and perfect. This pair of fake Vans and other fakes often just paint the stripe across the rubber to save cost. You can see the paint job here is not great; you can even see a dab of paint slopped onto the toe foxing.

Watch the outsole foxing tape

You can see where the toe tip rubber part is attached to the shoe on the authentic pair of Vans. Meanwhile, the counterfeit Vans sole has a very different surface texture, and the toe foxing is molded directly to the sole unit. This is very suspicious! This outsole may not have been made by vulcanization. On the authentic Vans shoe, you can see the tiny gap where these two parts come together. The authentic Vans toe tip is glued on, NOT molded together as one piece like the counterfeit Vans shoe.

Counterfeit Vans upper construction

Let's have a look at the real and the fake Vans upper details. Look at the back edge of the vamp where the shoelaces attach; you can see the counterfeit Vans has alignment nibs to help the workers assemble the shoe. These are fine in the scope of general shoe construction, but they are not included in the Old Skool. You can see the white "Jazz Stripe" on the fake shoe has the same "nibs" while the real Vans side stripe is free of the ugly notches. Now, look just below the stripe; you can see the real Vans shoe has a kink in the accent stitching line while the fake Vans shoe has a smooth curve in the stitching line. Looking at the heel view, you can see the real Vans has a smooth topline while the fake shoe has a central peak. You can also see more "nibs" on the fake red shoe's heel counter from the side view.

Toe profile

The toe profile of the genuine Vans skate shoe is very low. The vamp runs flat. The copy Vans shoe has a much more rounded toe.

The Vans outsole quirk

Vans makes outsoles with three layers of rubber foxing tape glued together. While the fake Vans in red may look cleaner, it's not correct. The real Vans rubber outsole shows how the layers of rubber foxing tape come together in a bulging pileup of overlapping parts. While this may look like poor shoemaking, it is authentic to Vans sneakers.

Watch for outsole inconsistencies

Look for the secret country code. Vans makes shoes in several countries, including China, Vietnam, and South America, and may also use more than one factory in each country. The real Vans shoes will have a letter code hidden in the diamond pattern. In this case, the fake sneaker does have the code, but it is often missing from others. Looking at the sole closely, you can see that this fake sole has other problems. The fake sole has rubber color bleeding over the white and gum rubber, while the real sole has a crisp edge. You can also see the fake sole has a strange straight line along the edge of the gum rubber perimeter. Finally, on the fake sole, you can see the indented areas of the waffle sole are not completely flat. This is because the fake Vans shoe is made using a cheap mold with lower quality standards. Poor workmanship is typical in molds used to make fake shoes.

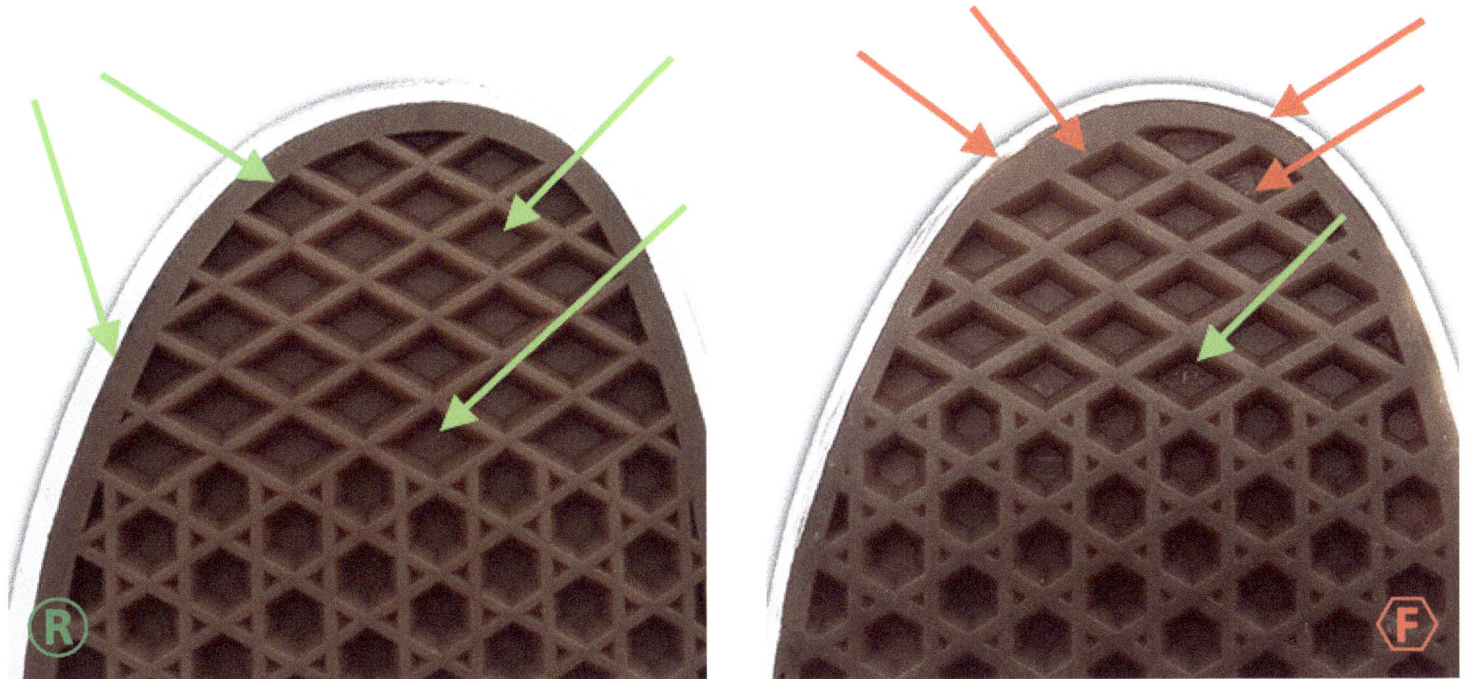

Giveaways inside the shoe

While you won't be able to cut your shoes open to authenticate, seeing the insides of these shoes is very important. Counterfeit shoes often take shortcuts on the inside of the shoe that customers don't see, which can ruin the shoe's integrity and hurt your feet. This fake pair of Vans has some huge problems. They are not made by the vulcanization process. The counterfeit Vans outsole is a one-piece rubber cupsole which is produced using the cold cement assembly process. The real Vans waffle sole is made from several assembled parts that have been bonded by vulcanization.

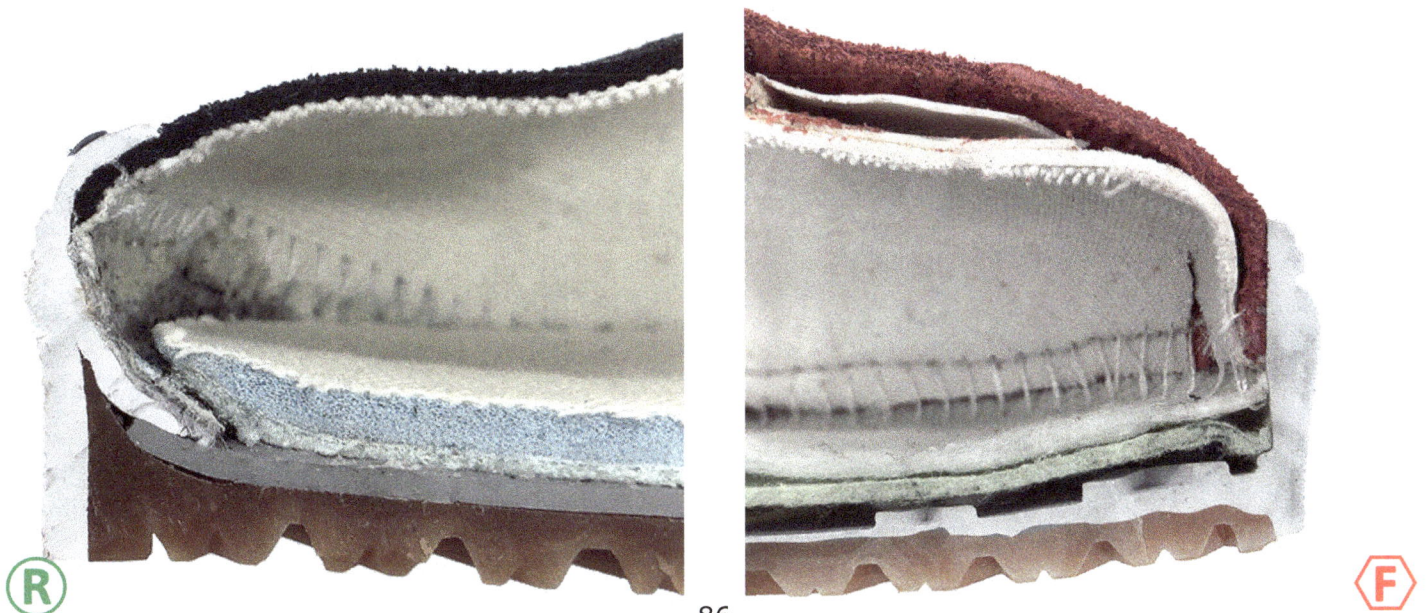

86

Vulcanization versus cold cement

In this cutaway section of the Vans shoes, you see blue and grey sponge rubber inside the real Vans shoe. The blue layer is a heat-resistant blow rubber sponge midsole. This cushioning material is formulated to withstand the heat of the vulcanizing oven. Also, to speed up production, the midsole is bonded to the lasting board. This reduces time required during assembly.

Inside the fake Vans, you see a green lasting board, a white Strobel layer, and an EVA footbed. The green board is glued in to stiffen the outsole. You can see the air gaps inside this shoe. These gaps mean the shoe is not securely bonded together.

Heel construction

Inside the heels of the shoes, you can see the fake shoe is made by Strobel construction. This process is not bad; it's just not how Vans classics are made. You don't have to cut open your shoes to check this feature—the real Vans shoe will have the footbed glued in securely. The counterfeit Vans may have a removable EVA footbed which is, in this case, a flat, die-cut piece of EVA. Being able to remove the footbed from the shoe is an easy tell that you are holding a fake pair of Old Skools.

One more thing to think about when evaluating the authenticity of a pair of Vans is the quality of the heel. Using your fingers, feel the inside of the heel. A well-made shoe will be nice and smooth, whereas a lower-quality fake shoe may be uneven and bumpy.

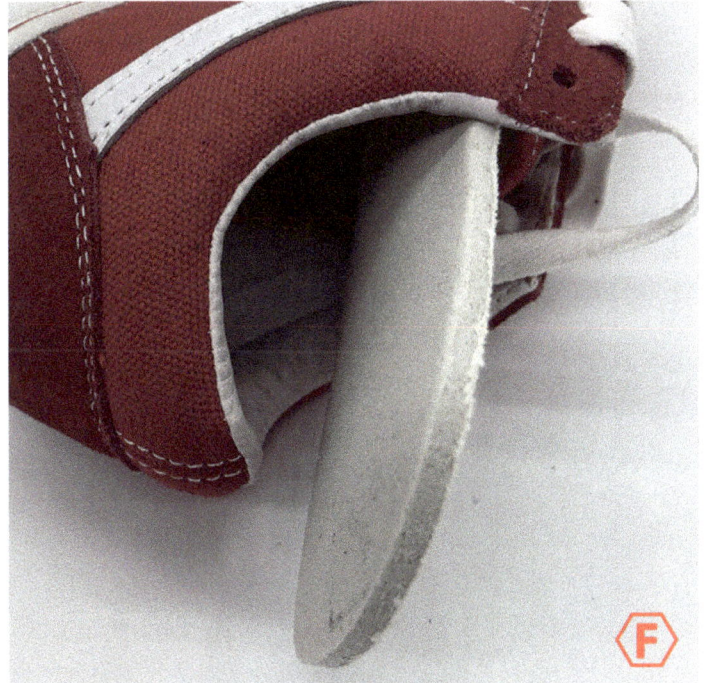

Closing

The Old Skool is easy to fake but very hard to fake well. Following this checklist is a great way to make sure you are looking at a real product. One thing to remember when authenticating Vans shoes is that many of them are deliberately imperfect. Don't let token quirks of Vans shoes, like the weird heel logo, cloud your judgment. You are comparing it to other shoes of the same model, not a perfectly made shoe.

Authentic Vans Old Skool

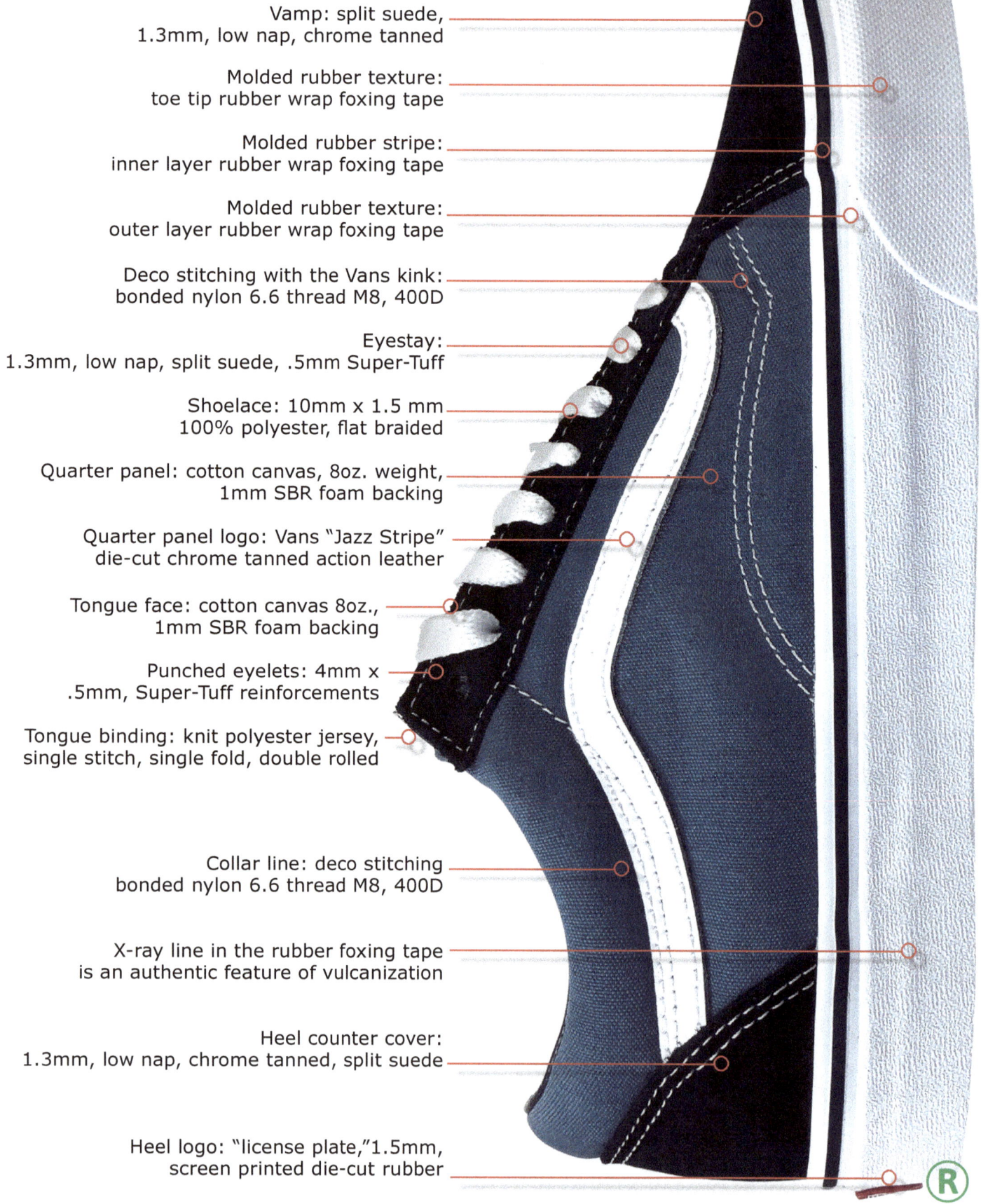

Vamp: split suede,
1.3mm, low nap, chrome tanned

Molded rubber texture:
toe tip rubber wrap foxing tape

Molded rubber stripe:
inner layer rubber wrap foxing tape

Molded rubber texture:
outer layer rubber wrap foxing tape

Deco stitching with the Vans kink:
bonded nylon 6.6 thread M8, 400D

Eyestay:
1.3mm, low nap, split suede, .5mm Super-Tuff

Shoelace: 10mm x 1.5 mm
100% polyester, flat braided

Quarter panel: cotton canvas, 8oz. weight,
1mm SBR foam backing

Quarter panel logo: Vans "Jazz Stripe"
die-cut chrome tanned action leather

Tongue face: cotton canvas 8oz.,
1mm SBR foam backing

Punched eyelets: 4mm x
.5mm, Super-Tuff reinforcements

Tongue binding: knit polyester jersey,
single stitch, single fold, double rolled

Collar line: deco stitching
bonded nylon 6.6 thread M8, 400D

X-ray line in the rubber foxing tape
is an authentic feature of vulcanization

Heel counter cover:
1.3mm, low nap, chrome tanned, split suede

Heel logo: "license plate,"1.5mm,
screen printed die-cut rubber

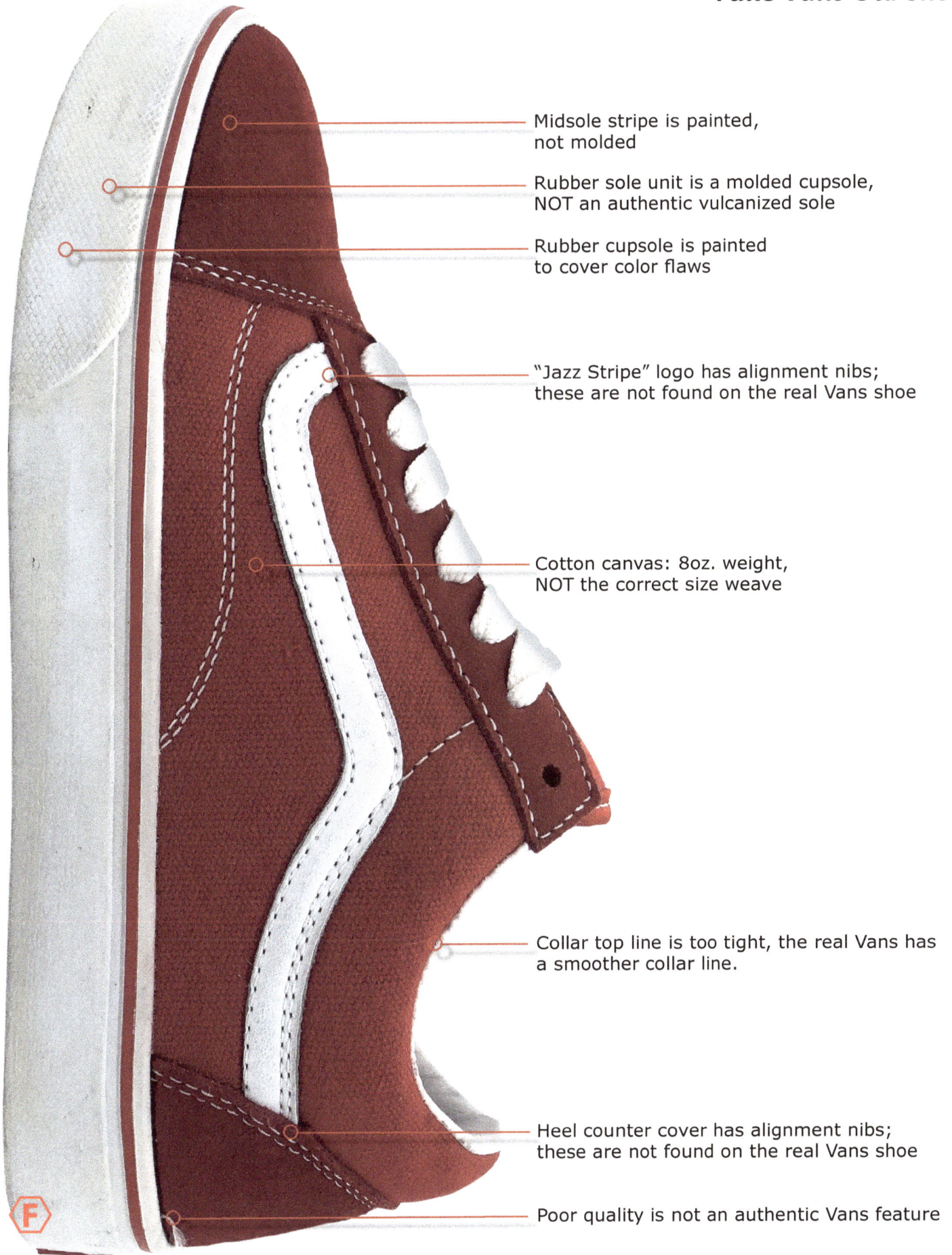

Midsole stripe is painted, not molded

Rubber sole unit is a molded cupsole, NOT an authentic vulcanized sole

Rubber cupsole is painted to cover color flaws

"Jazz Stripe" logo has alignment nibs; these are not found on the real Vans shoe

Cotton canvas: 8oz. weight, NOT the correct size weave

Collar top line is too tight, the real Vans has a smoother collar line.

Heel counter cover has alignment nibs; these are not found on the real Vans shoe

Poor quality is not an authentic Vans feature

Authentic Vans Old Skool

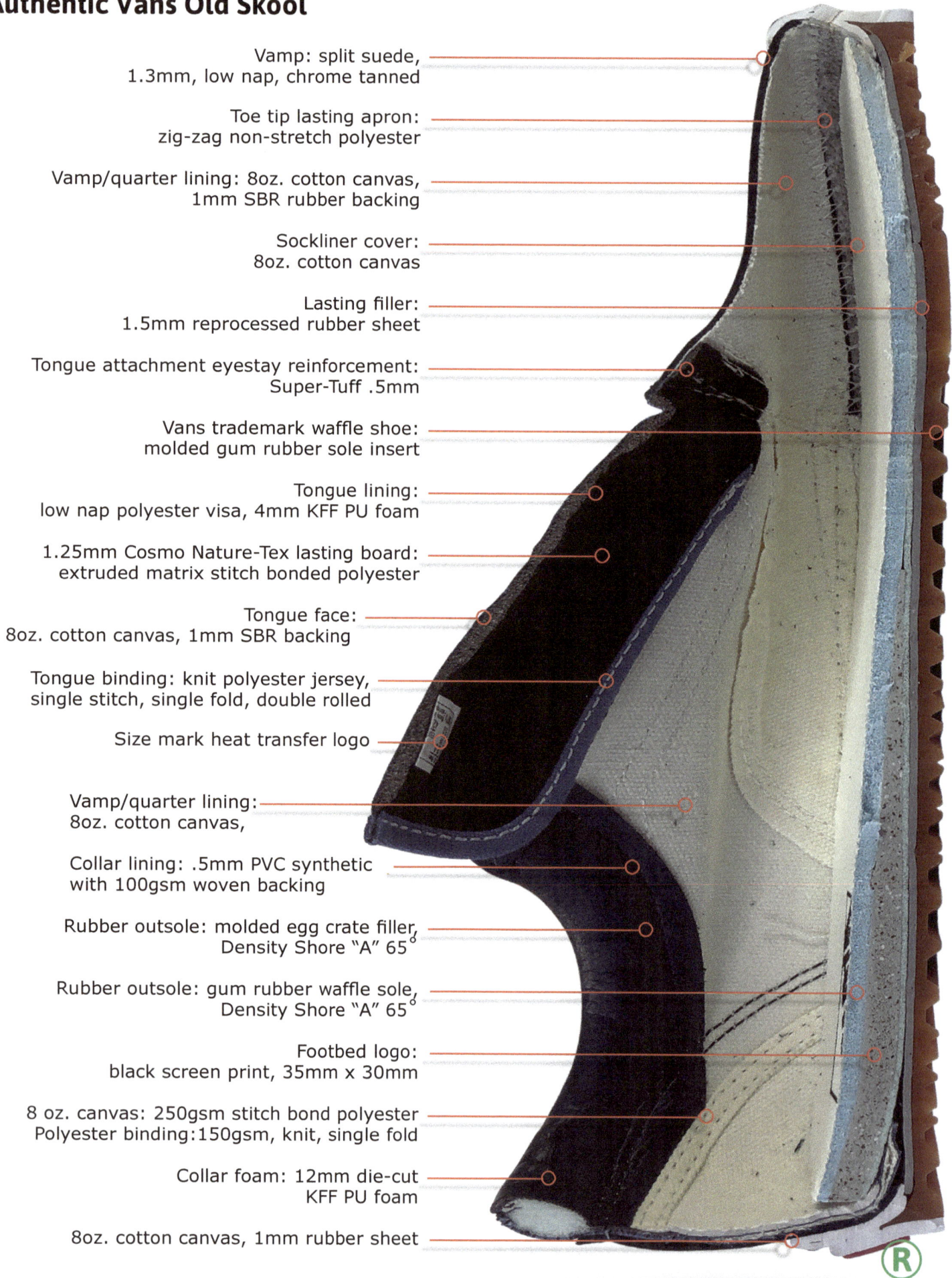

Vamp: split suede,
1.3mm, low nap, chrome tanned

Toe tip lasting apron:
zig-zag non-stretch polyester

Vamp/quarter lining: 8oz. cotton canvas,
1mm SBR rubber backing

Sockliner cover:
8oz. cotton canvas

Lasting filler:
1.5mm reprocessed rubber sheet

Tongue attachment eyestay reinforcement:
Super-Tuff .5mm

Vans trademark waffle shoe:
molded gum rubber sole insert

Tongue lining:
low nap polyester visa, 4mm KFF PU foam

1.25mm Cosmo Nature-Tex lasting board:
extruded matrix stitch bonded polyester

Tongue face:
8oz. cotton canvas, 1mm SBR backing

Tongue binding: knit polyester jersey,
single stitch, single fold, double rolled

Size mark heat transfer logo

Vamp/quarter lining:
8oz. cotton canvas,

Collar lining: .5mm PVC synthetic
with 100gsm woven backing

Rubber outsole: molded egg crate filler,
Density Shore "A" 65°

Rubber outsole: gum rubber waffle sole,
Density Shore "A" 65°

Footbed logo:
black screen print, 35mm x 30mm

8 oz. canvas: 250gsm stitch bond polyester
Polyester binding:150gsm, knit, single fold

Collar foam: 12mm die-cut
KFF PU foam

8oz. cotton canvas, 1mm rubber sheet

®

Fake Vans Old Skool

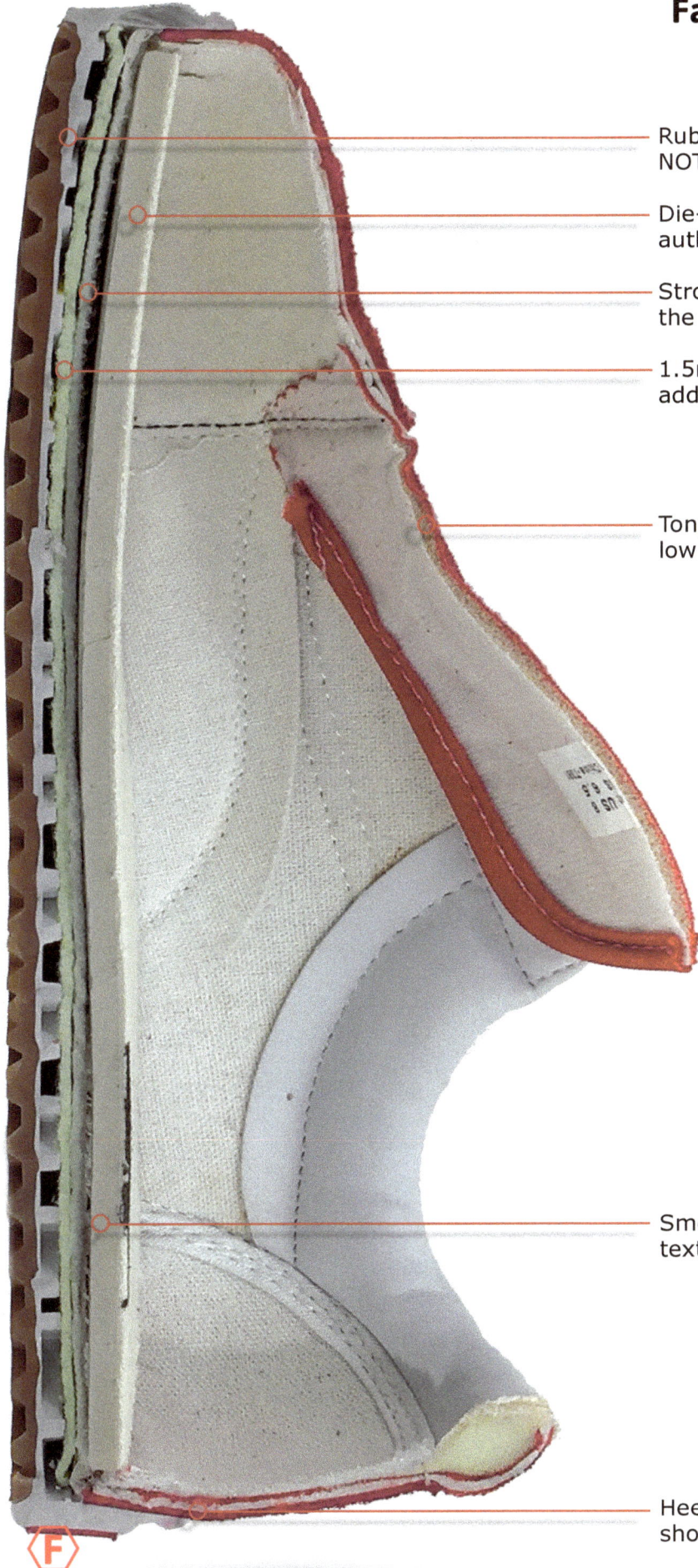

Rubber sole unit is a molded cupsole,
NOT an authentic vulcanized sole

Die-cut EVA footbed: 6mm is not correct,
authentic Vans has sponge rubber cushioning

Strobel sock is not correct,
the authentic Vans Old Skool is board-lasted

1.5mm Cosmo Nature-Tex lasting board:
added to stiffen the cupsole

Tongue foam:
low quality (too thin)

Smooth PVC collar lining:
texture is wrong

Heel counter is 1.0mm Chemo sheet,
should be rubber sheet

Chapter 10 : How to Spot a Fake Nike Air Max 90

Originally known as the Air Max III, The Air Max 90 was renamed in 2000, taking its name from the year of its original launch. When Nike released the Air Max 90, it was a state-of-the-art running shoe with a revolutionary design.

With the introduction of the giant air cell, rubber badges, and unique upper design, Nike finally cast aside the more conventional styling of the Air Max 1 ('87) and V Series ('84 to '86) running shoes.

The Air Max 90 left the stage when Nike introduced the very forgettable Air Max Light in 1989.

The Air Max 90 today

Thirty years later, the Air Max 90 is now a staple of Nike's re-released classics overshadowing the many less memorable Air Max models that followed. Of course, being an iconic long-running model has made the Air Max 90 the target of counterfeiters worldwide.

The upper design is a simple cut and sew with a few flat molded parts. These are inexpensive to tool up and not expensive to produce. The PU with airbag midsole was once state of the art, but this technology is now commonplace in the modern shoe factory.

You can find Air Max 90 copies and clones in shoe stores from the urban centers of mainland China to the Zapaterias of rural Mexico.

Authenticating the Nike Air Max 90
What to look for

Construction details

Counterfeiters do their best to make the fake shoe "look" authentic but they can't duplicate the construction and will not pay for the high quality sub components. The Air Max 90 has many small parts to study, we will find that piece-by-piece the fake shoe falls short of the original.

Check the three part outsole, you should see
#1 a molded PU midsole
#2 a two-color rubber sole
#3 the airbag

The molded upper parts should be a tough flexible plastic. Soft stretchable rubber parts are a bad sign.

Nike has their way of doing things. They put two ® logos on the tongue. It's strange but correct.

Counterfeiters make strange mistakes. They may put too many support pillars in an air bag. Every detail is important, look carefully.

All shoes are made by humans - even the legendary Air Max 90 Infrared. So, even an authentic shoe may have some sloppy paint.

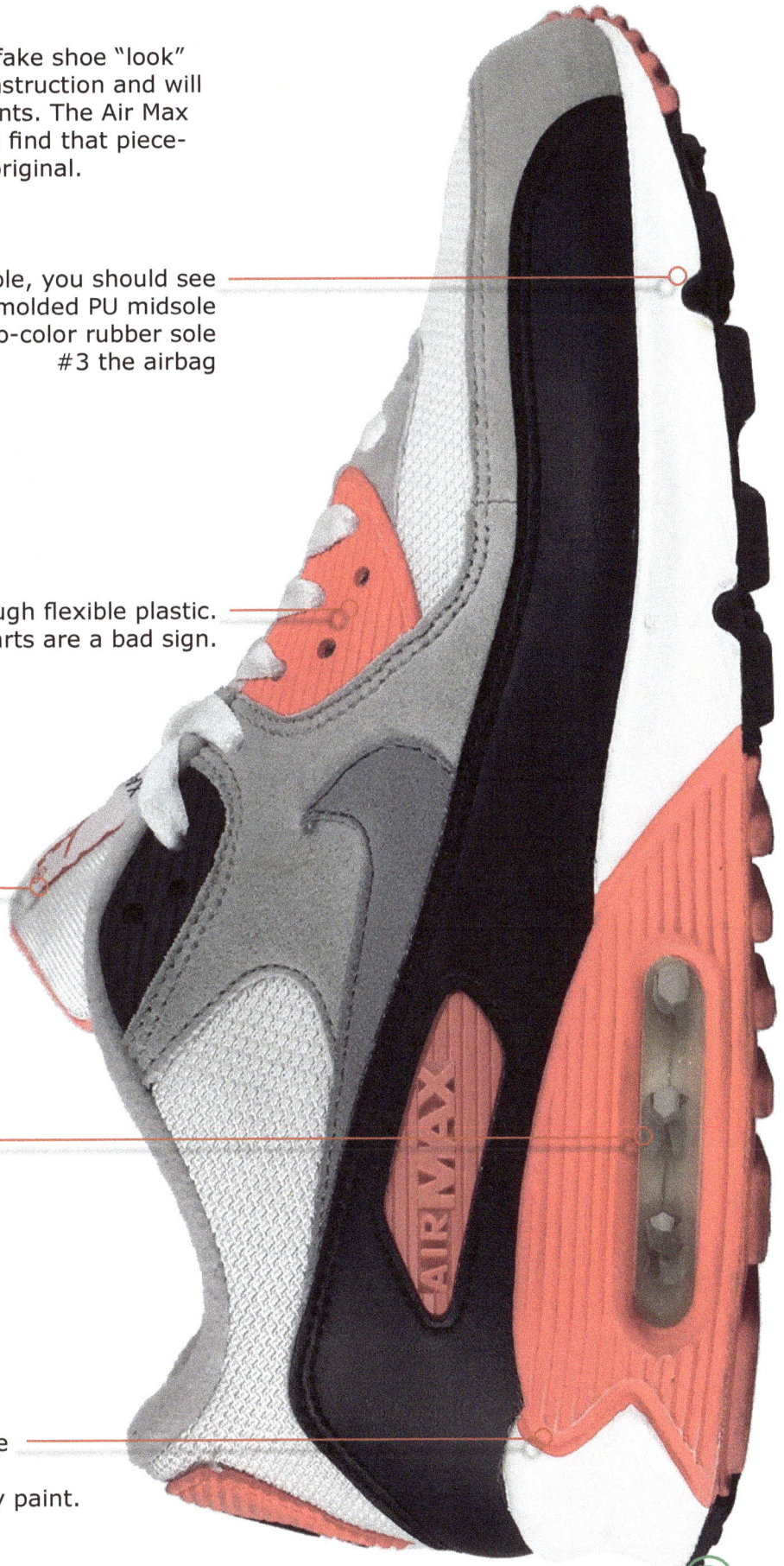

First, look at the shoe bottom

The outsole on the real (red) pair of Air Max 90s is made of rubber, while the blue pair has an outsole made of painted PU foam. I also noticed the fake blue sneaker weighs much less than the authentic red Nike sneaker. If you look closely, the blue shoe is even missing the Nike logo.

Many fraudulent companies make fakes; some are better imitators than others. Here are some differences that you can use to distinguish between real and fake Nike Air Max 90s.

(R)

(F)

Check out the tongue logo

Our real shoe has the "Nike+Swoosh" label sewn down on all four sides. The fake is turned and stitched into the tongue seam. While this is a nicer way to attach the tongue logo, it doesn't follow the original Nike construction. Take another look at the artwork. On the real patch, the tail of the swoosh overlaps the "E" of Nike, and the head of the swoosh almost touches the "N." Notice the fake label has the "Air" logo twice.

Most fake Nike shoes will have the circled "R" to signify registration, don't let that convince you a Nike shoe is real. There is nothing to stop the fake shoe factory from adding the "TM" trademark logo either.

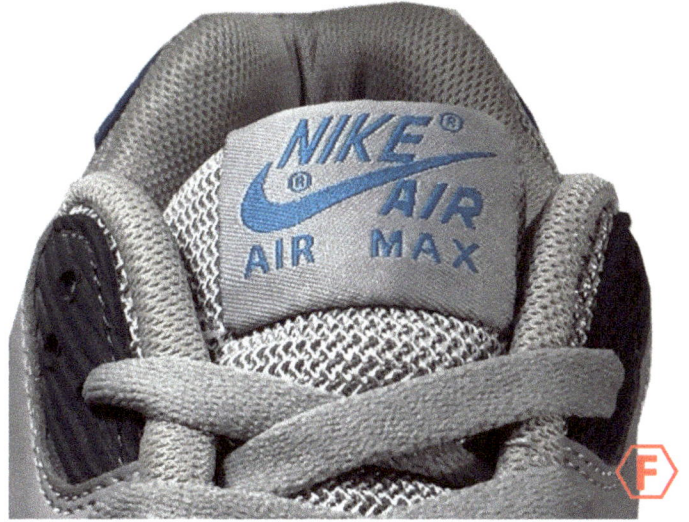

Look at the heel logo

On our fake Air Max 90, the stitching groove interferes with the "A" and the "R" of the Nike Air logo. Also, the counterfeit shoe "Air" logo is missing the molded ribs below the letters. Additionally, the top shape of the original Nike patch has a significant dip in the middle.

Examine the side Air Max logo

Our counterfeit Nike has a two-tone logo, while the real deal Nike has a single color. When you feel the logo, the authentic Nike Air Max logo is made of stiff plastic due to its location on the shoe being

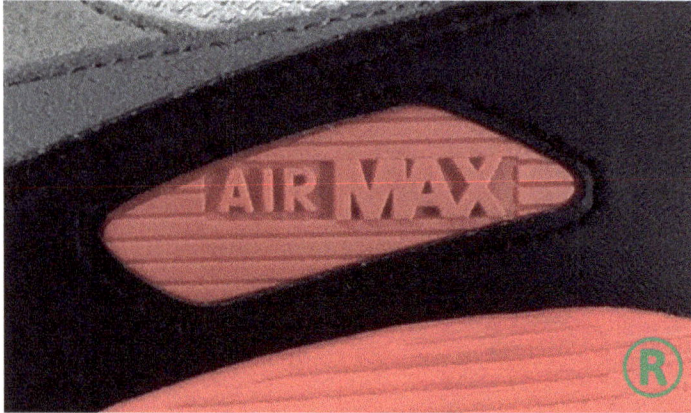

just above the outsole, while the fake logo is a softer material that was distorted during the shoe assembly process. In addition, the original logo is made by plastic injection in comparison to the soft PVC logo on the fake shoe.

Watch the paint around the airbag in the heel

While the Air Max original paintwork isn't perfect, the fake Nike paintwork is a mess with paint outside the lines.

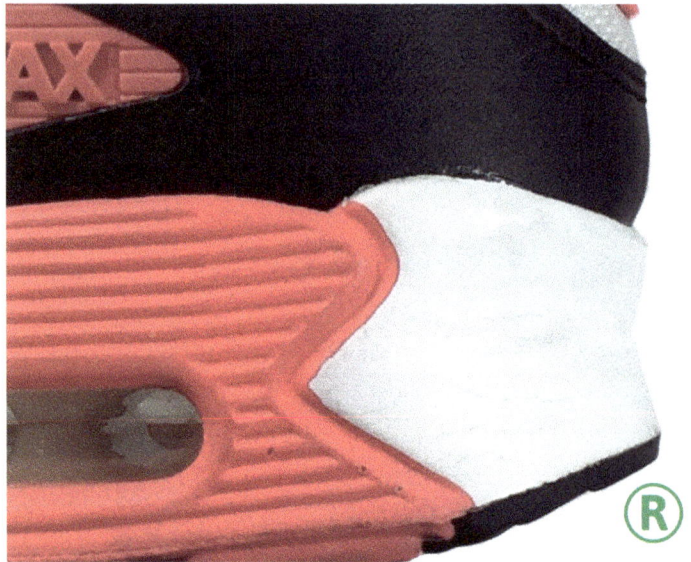

These pieces are generally hand-painted so even the paint job on authentic Nike footwear won't always be perfect. If a genuine pair has a bad paint job, Nike itself may choose not to sell it, or if you encounter a pair in a store, you can just ask for a new one.

Look inside at the footbed

The original Nike shoe has a 3D compression-molded EVA footbed with the outsole design pattern and printed logo. The counterfeit Air Max 90 has a super cheap die-cut foam sheet.

Looking at the footbed can often be a very easy way to spot fakes. The footbed is often overlooked by people creating the forgeries as well as the people buying them. Some shoes have glued-in footbeds, while forgeries may have removable ones, make sure to keep an eye out.

Compare the midsole constructions

The real Nike midsole is made of supple and solid but flexible PU foam, while the fake is made of a much cheaper, more rigid form. So the shoe still bends like an original. To save money on the cheaper foam, you can see part of the foam on the fake shoes is unfilled.

This fake has a circular pattern hidden in the midsole to save on foam. The Strobel sock on the fake is barely even glued.

You can also see the fake shoe is missing the forefoot flex notches on the midsole sidewall.

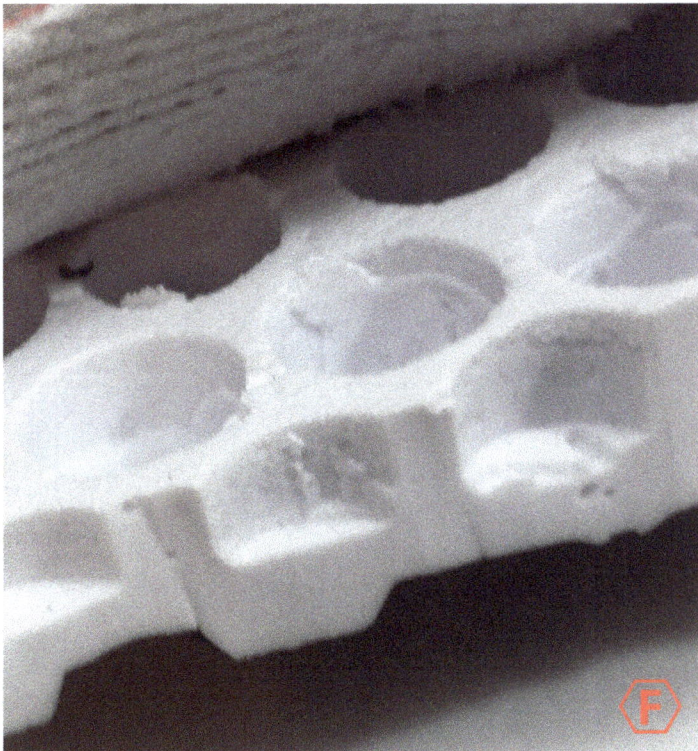

Examine the airbag

The genuine Nike shoe has a thin film blow-molded airbag with three cells. The fake Nike has a thicker walled, stiffer airbag. Notice the different colors of the airbag materials. Nike uses a special formula to keep the air in, which creates a yellow tint, while the fake is made of clear PVC plastic. Not to mention the size differences and the fact that the fake shoe has an extra air bubble. While the extra bubble is harder to spot on the shoe before it's cut up, it is visible and a dead giveaway.

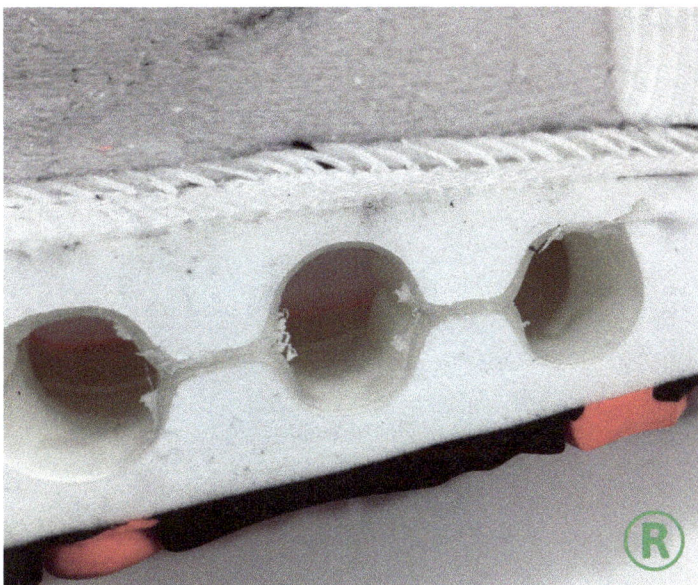

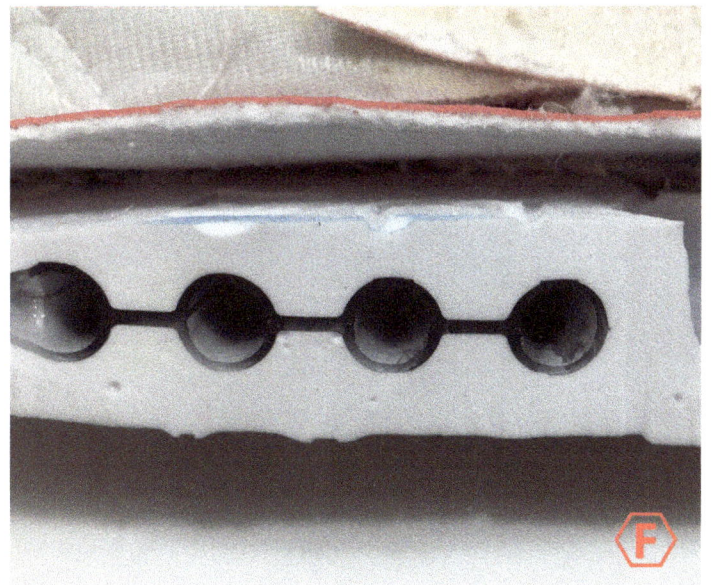

Find the sizing and SKU numbers

Remember to look at the barcode and SKU numbers. Every pair of real Nike shoes has an SKU (pronounced "skew") or Stock Keeping Number identical to the SKU number on the box. If the numbers are missing or do not match, you may have a fake shoe.

Check the tongue label. Often, the counterfeiting shoe factory will put outdated size labels on the inside of the shoe. The label information may be incorrect as well, so keep an eye out.

Feel the tongue of the shoe

Inside the real Nike, you find an extra layer of foam that's missing from the fake shoe. Depending on the quality of the fake, you will be able to feel a tangible difference between the shoes.

It will be hard to feel at the tip -where people often touch, but further down the tongue, the missing foam becomes more obvious.

Look at the upper reinforcements

The authentic Nike has grey non-woven "super tuff" fabric backing the top eyelet holes. The fake Nike does not have any reinforcement.

While the picture shows a cut-up shoe, you can stick your finger between the seams and feel the difference yourself pretty easily without cutting open the shoe.

Look deeper inside

Peel back the lining to find more differences between the real and fake shoe. While both shoes use a similar plastic-infused paperboard for the heel counter, you can see the fake one doesn't fit well, and the edges have not been skived down.

Look at the midsole heel of the fake—what a mess! While this is hidden by fabric on the inside of the shoe, you will never find a quality branded shoe that looks like the messy fake shoe we have here.

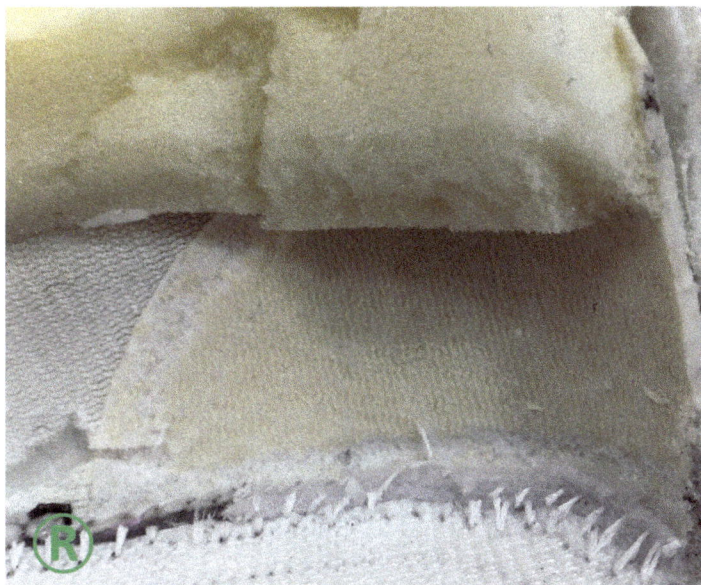

Look at the toe tip area inside the shoe

The original Nike shoe has even, closely spaced stitches, while the copy has loose, uneven, and widely spaced stitches.

The fake shoe was not carefully made, and the toe lasting operation has left a junk show inside. Look at the spacing of the Strobel stitches that hold the upper to the bottom.

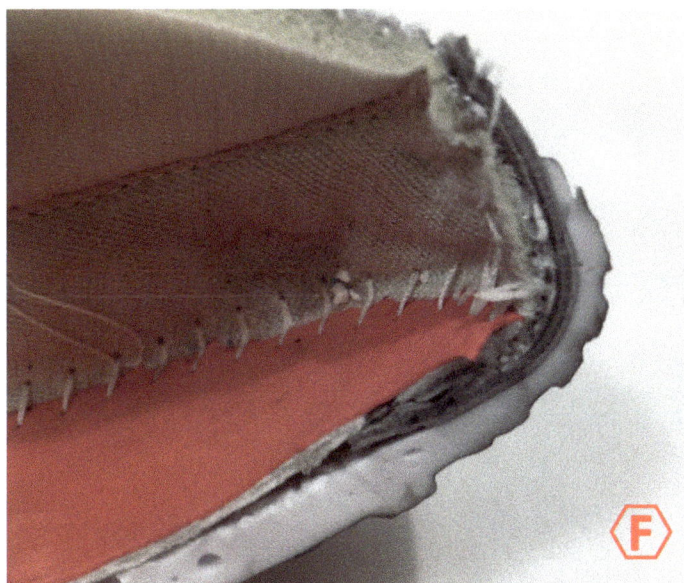

Do your research

In this case, our Nike Air Max 90 counterfeit is really a rotten shoe. You can see that not only are the design details of the fake incorrect, but the internal construction is really terrible as well. So, while the fake shoe may look pretty good on the outside, the inside is a horror show of low-quality shoemaking.

The Authentic Nike Air Max 90

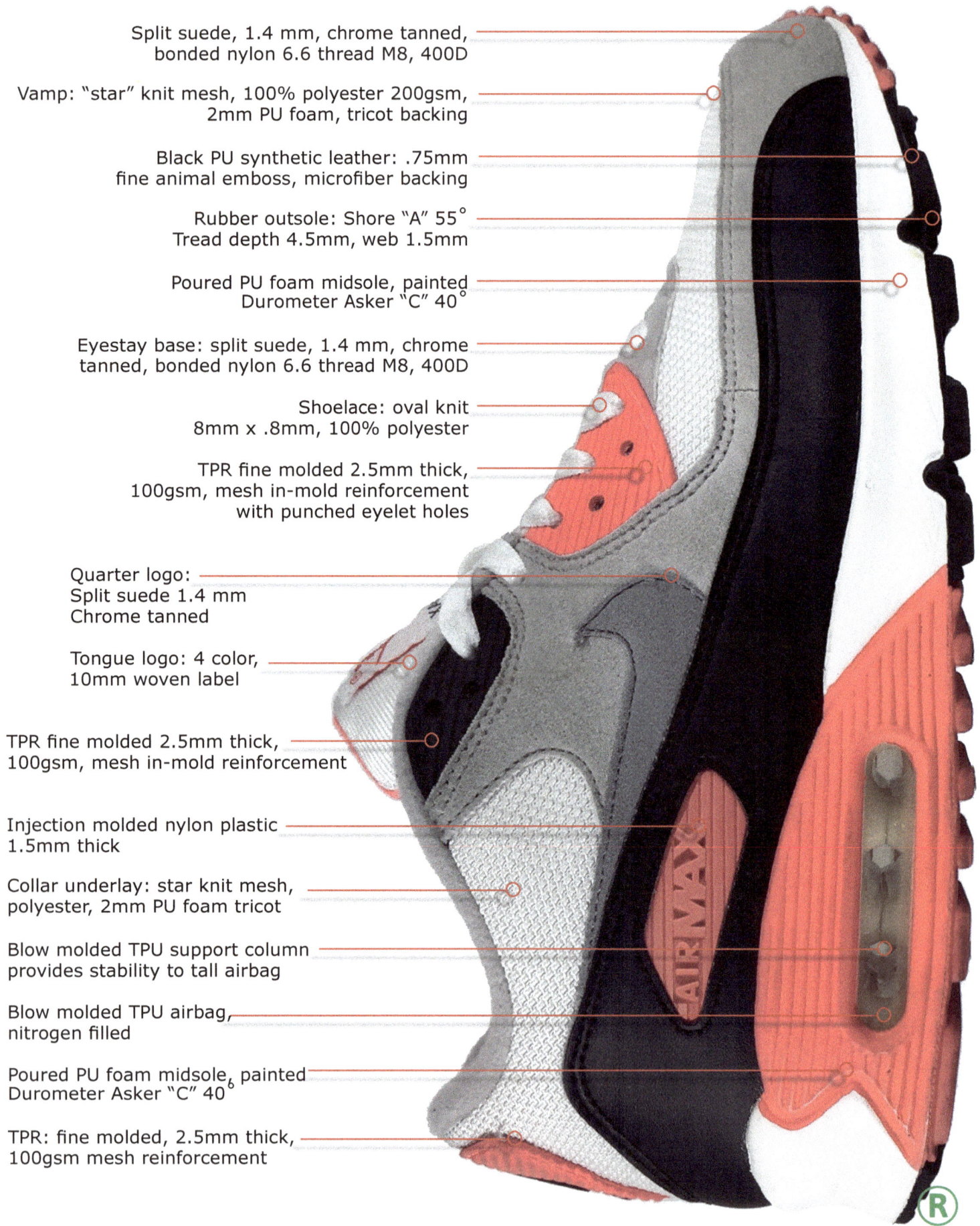

Split suede, 1.4 mm, chrome tanned,
bonded nylon 6.6 thread M8, 400D

Vamp: "star" knit mesh, 100% polyester 200gsm,
2mm PU foam, tricot backing

Black PU synthetic leather: .75mm
fine animal emboss, microfiber backing

Rubber outsole: Shore "A" 55°
Tread depth 4.5mm, web 1.5mm

Poured PU foam midsole, painted
Durometer Asker "C" 40°

Eyestay base: split suede, 1.4 mm, chrome
tanned, bonded nylon 6.6 thread M8, 400D

Shoelace: oval knit
8mm x .8mm, 100% polyester

TPR fine molded 2.5mm thick,
100gsm, mesh in-mold reinforcement
with punched eyelet holes

Quarter logo:
Split suede 1.4 mm
Chrome tanned

Tongue logo: 4 color,
10mm woven label

TPR fine molded 2.5mm thick,
100gsm, mesh in-mold reinforcement

Injection molded nylon plastic
1.5mm thick

Collar underlay: star knit mesh,
polyester, 2mm PU foam tricot

Blow molded TPU support column
provides stability to tall airbag

Blow molded TPU airbag,
nitrogen filled

Poured PU foam midsole, painted
Durometer Asker "C" 40°

TPR: fine molded, 2.5mm thick,
100gsm mesh reinforcement

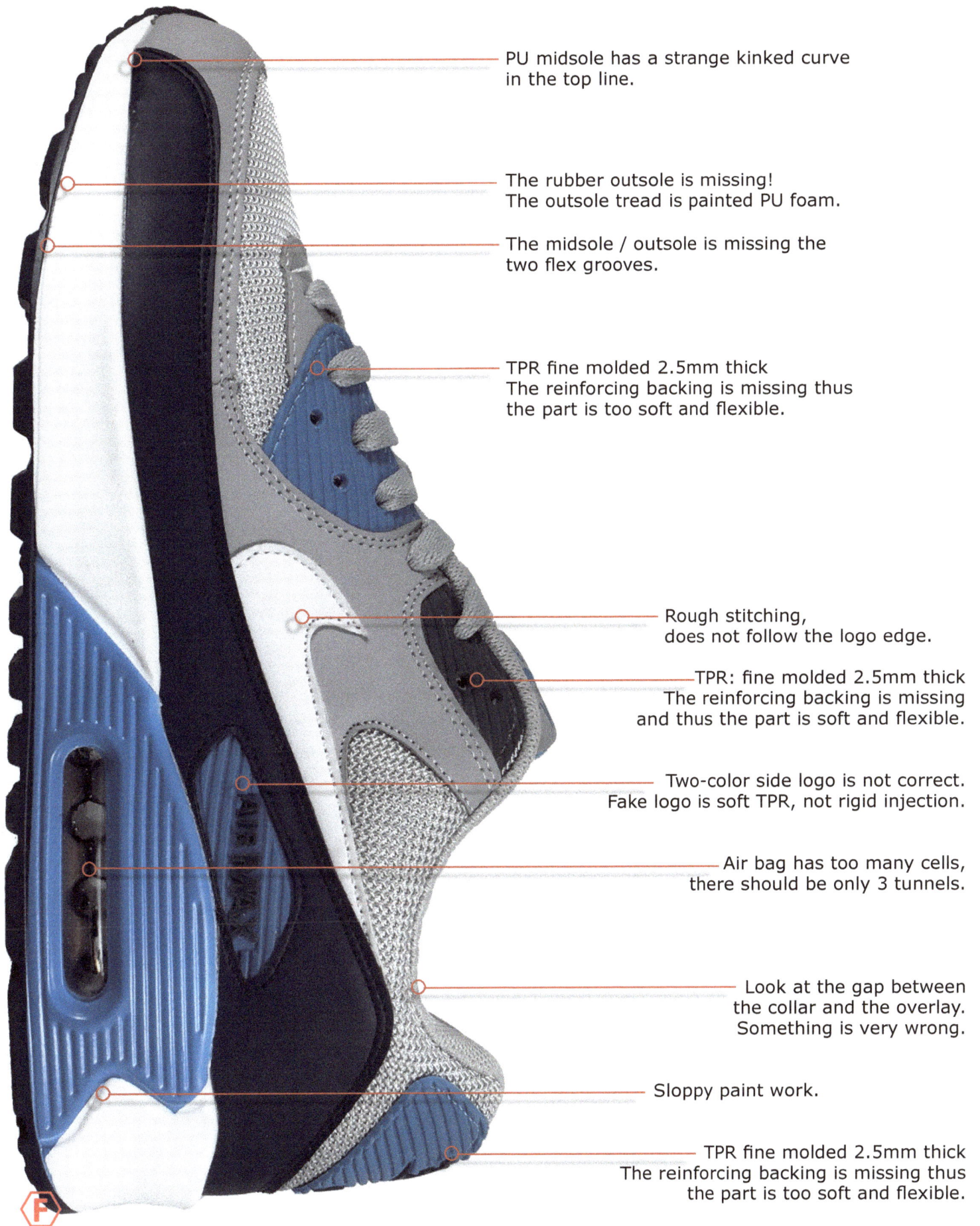

PU midsole has a strange kinked curve in the top line.

The rubber outsole is missing! The outsole tread is painted PU foam.

The midsole / outsole is missing the two flex grooves.

TPR fine molded 2.5mm thick The reinforcing backing is missing thus the part is too soft and flexible.

Rough stitching, does not follow the logo edge.

TPR: fine molded 2.5mm thick The reinforcing backing is missing and thus the part is soft and flexible.

Two-color side logo is not correct. Fake logo is soft TPR, not rigid injection.

Air bag has too many cells, there should be only 3 tunnels.

Look at the gap between the collar and the overlay. Something is very wrong.

Sloppy paint work.

TPR fine molded 2.5mm thick The reinforcing backing is missing thus the part is too soft and flexible.

Inside the real Nike Air Max 90

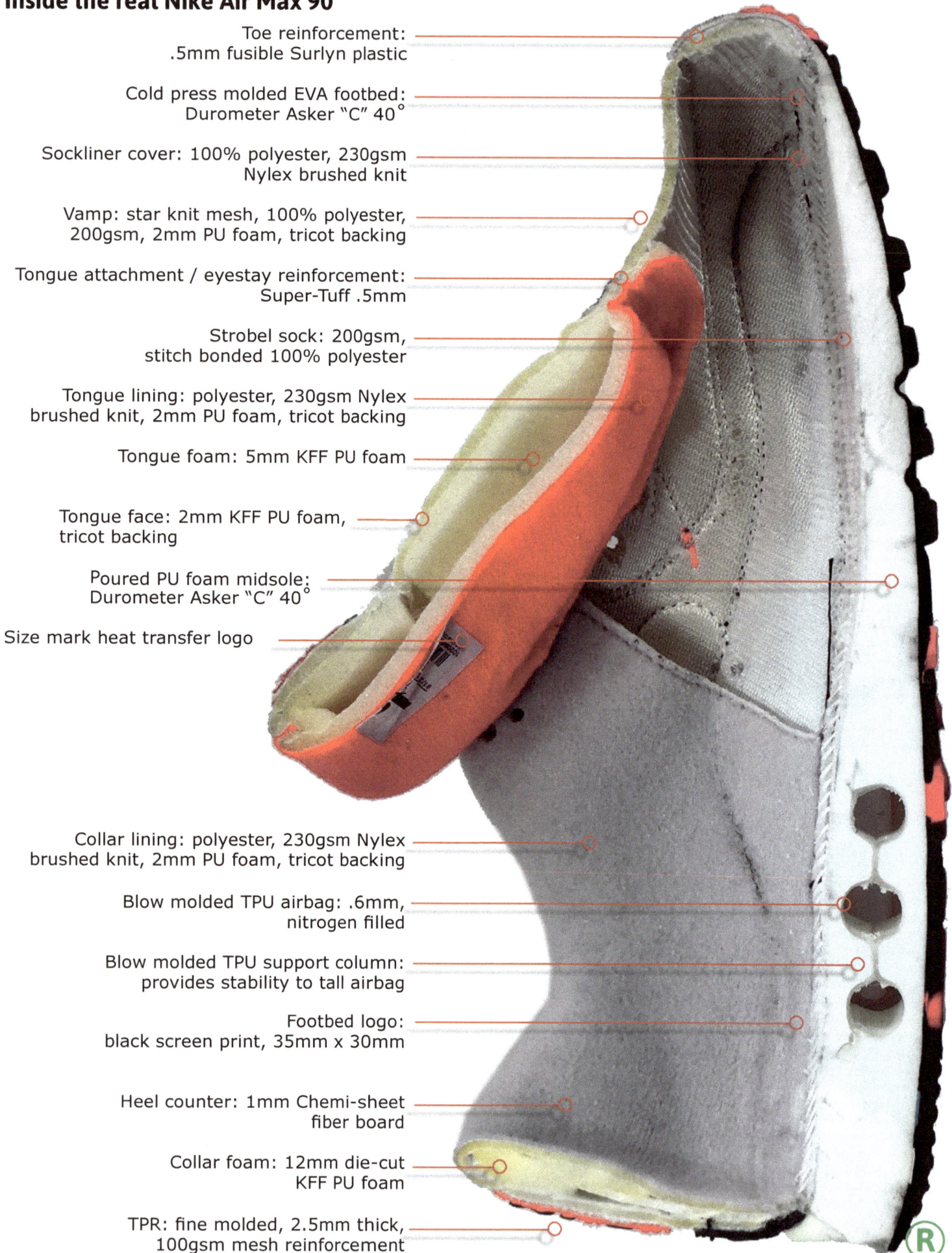

Toe reinforcement:
.5mm fusible Surlyn plastic

Cold press molded EVA footbed:
Durometer Asker "C" 40°

Sockliner cover: 100% polyester, 230gsm
Nylex brushed knit

Vamp: star knit mesh, 100% polyester,
200gsm, 2mm PU foam, tricot backing

Tongue attachment / eyestay reinforcement:
Super-Tuff .5mm

Strobel sock: 200gsm,
stitch bonded 100% polyester

Tongue lining: polyester, 230gsm Nylex
brushed knit, 2mm PU foam, tricot backing

Tongue foam: 5mm KFF PU foam

Tongue face: 2mm KFF PU foam,
tricot backing

Poured PU foam midsole:
Durometer Asker "C" 40°

Size mark heat transfer logo

Collar lining: polyester, 230gsm Nylex
brushed knit, 2mm PU foam, tricot backing

Blow molded TPU airbag: .6mm,
nitrogen filled

Blow molded TPU support column:
provides stability to tall airbag

Footbed logo:
black screen print, 35mm x 30mm

Heel counter: 1mm Chemi-sheet
fiber board

Collar foam: 12mm die-cut
KFF PU foam

TPR: fine molded, 2.5mm thick,
100gsm mesh reinforcement

®

Inside the fake Nike Air Max 90

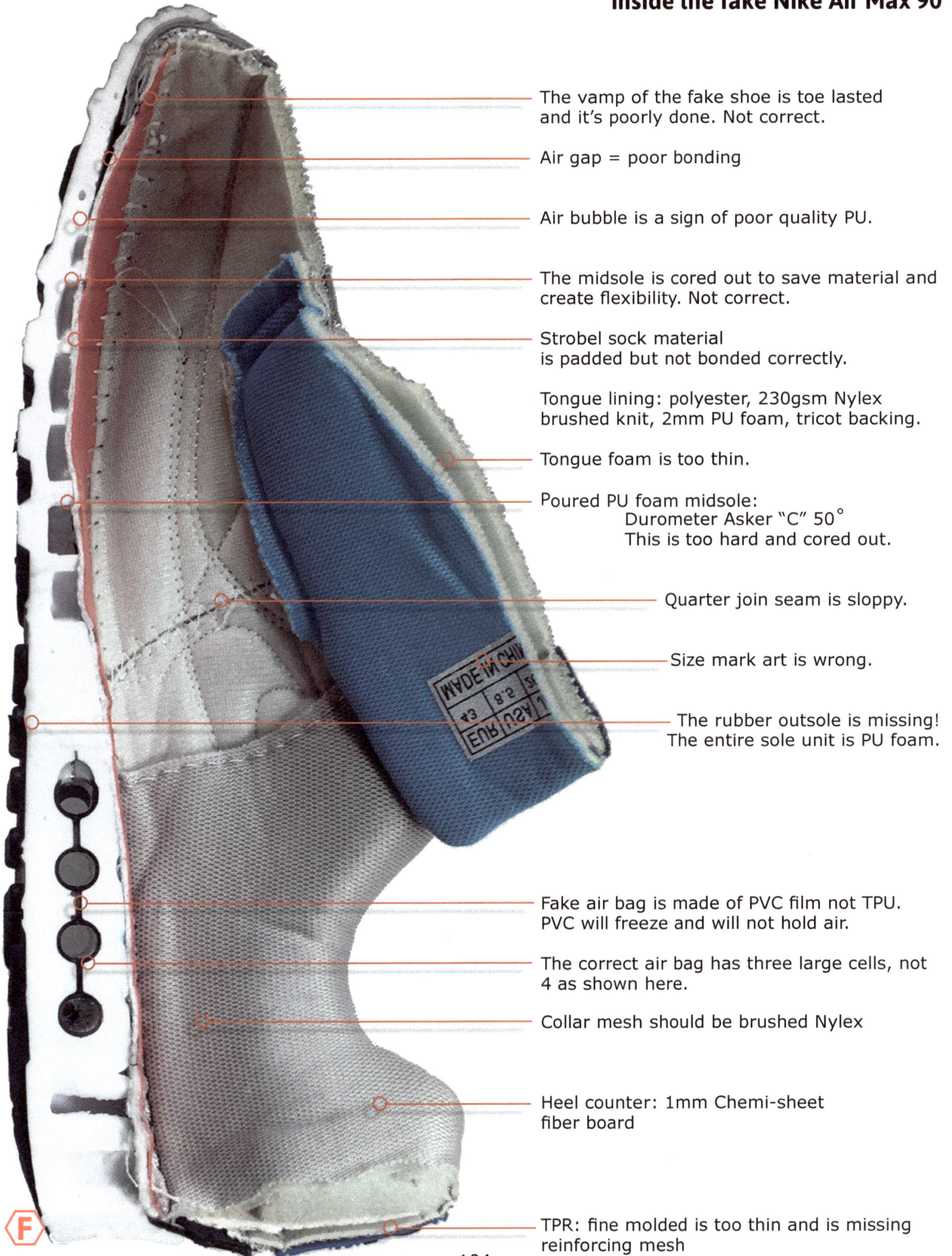

The vamp of the fake shoe is toe lasted and it's poorly done. Not correct.

Air gap = poor bonding

Air bubble is a sign of poor quality PU.

The midsole is cored out to save material and create flexibility. Not correct.

Strobel sock material is padded but not bonded correctly.

Tongue lining: polyester, 230gsm Nylex brushed knit, 2mm PU foam, tricot backing.

Tongue foam is too thin.

Poured PU foam midsole:
    Durometer Asker "C" 50°
    This is too hard and cored out.

Quarter join seam is sloppy.

Size mark art is wrong.

The rubber outsole is missing! The entire sole unit is PU foam.

Fake air bag is made of PVC film not TPU. PVC will freeze and will not hold air.

The correct air bag has three large cells, not 4 as shown here.

Collar mesh should be brushed Nylex

Heel counter: 1mm Chemi-sheet fiber board

TPR: fine molded is too thin and is missing reinforcing mesh

Chapter 11: How to Spot a Fake Nike Daybreak

The Classic Jogger

The Nike Daybreak is one of the original shoes created by the mastermind Bill Bowerman. The Daybreak's simple design became the pattern for all running shoes. Its iconic design DNA can be found in the newest Nike performance running shoes.

The 1979 design of the Daybreak is functionally obsolete, but its sleek styling has made it a retro fashion staple.

It's the Daybeak's icon status and fashion appeal that has attracted the attention of counterfeiters. The simple sheet cut construction of the outsole requires very little tooling so the Daybreak looks like an easy mark for duplication.

We will see in this chapter, the 1970's Daybreak design is not so easy to make. Nike has done an excellent job replicating the design with modern manufacturing techniques. The 2022 version is made to a much higher standard than the original.

Authenticating the Nike Daybreak
What to look for

Silhouette

The Daybreak is such a simple shoe and its sleek silhouette is the dominating feature. The functional parts are applied to the textile base with few overlapping sections to obscure the shoe's profile.

The profiled midsole cross-section and ultra-thin outsole web are prominently exposed. The upper is pulled down tight, creating its iconic sleek shape. Counterfeiters do not take the time to get these aspects of the Daybreak correct.

Look for the sleek down sloping vamp.

The outsole web is thin and straight.

High-nap fuzzy suede is correct.

Clean cut edges are free of alignment marks.

The upper is pulled down and tucks tight to the midsole.

The collar line is crisp and padding is thin.

The EVA midsole flares out, the bottom is wider than the top.

The heel counter is sleek and firm with an ergonomic heel cupping contour.

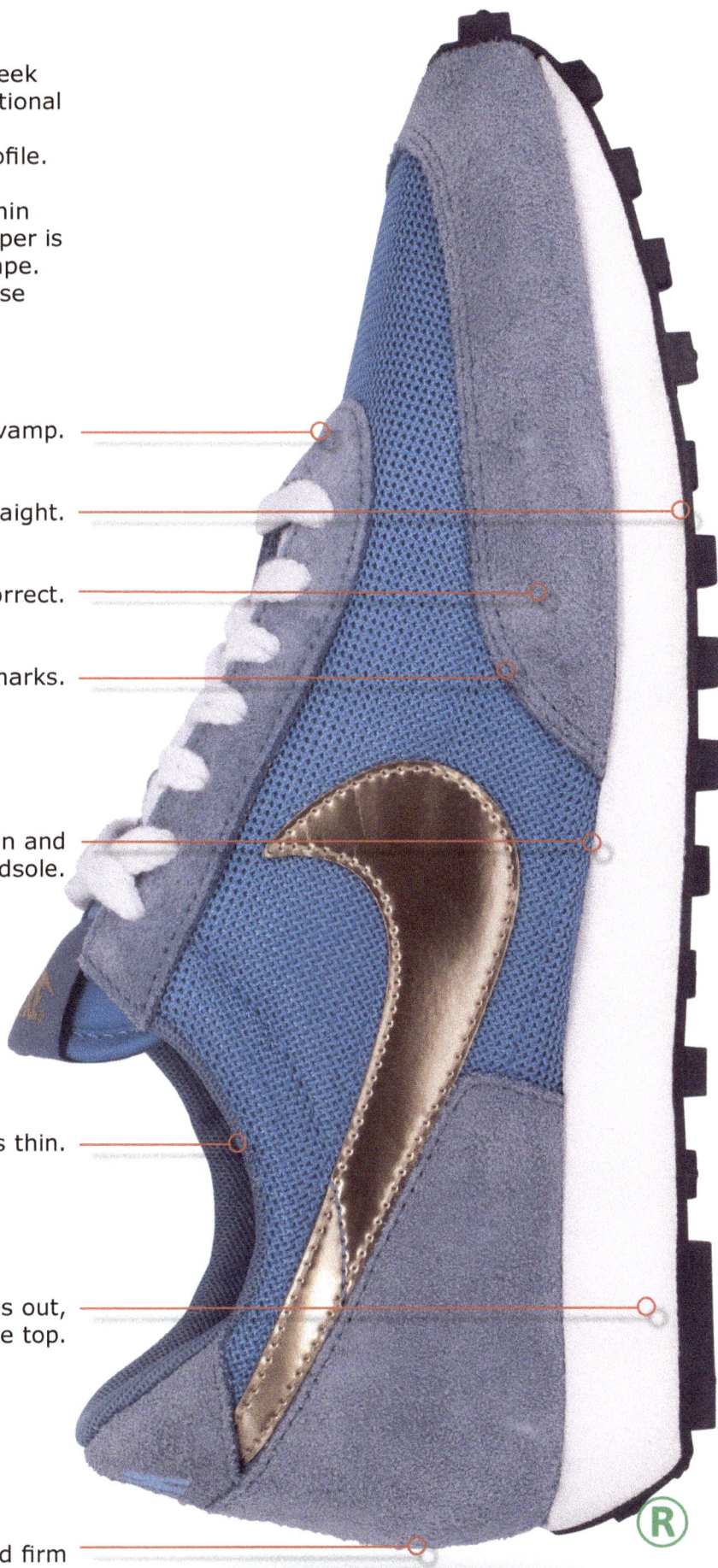

Nike Daybreak materials

The original 1979 Nike Daybreak was made with shiny 110D nylon and hairy suede. The 2019 re-release has a significant upgrade of breathable polyester 3D air mesh with a smooth inside face that makes the shoe lining. The suede of the re-release is authentic almost to a fault. Looking at the real shoe (top photo) and the fake (bottom photo), you might mistake the fake shoe's smooth, low-nap suede, as correct. It's not. Also, the real Nike Daybreak has a faded blue hue; this is correct.

The mesh surface of the fake shoe is similar, but when you look inside, you will see the backing surface is not color matched.

Tongue logo

The woven label on the real Daybreak is not a perfect rendering of the official Nike + Swoosh logo. The double ® trademark symbol is correct. What we are looking for in the woven label is quality. The real Nike label is smooth and flat with tight stitching. The fake logo has longer stitches with some buckling in the "N," "K," and "E." The "E" is also missing the step down to the tail of the swoosh.

Make sure to look at the back of the label. It should be blank. In this case, you can see the tail end of the logo on the fake was missed by the stitcher. You can see the extra-long tail of the logo hanging.
See the fake Daybreak cross-section for more details.

The quarter swoosh logo

The Nike Swoosh is a simple die-cut logo design that counterfeiters cannot seem to get right. The human brain has developed an amazing aptitude for pattern recognition. We have seen the correct logo so many times that when we see a logo with even mild distortions it is off-putting. In this case, the shape of the logo is obviously wrong, as is the foil like glossy surface of the gold synthetic leather.

The Daybreak pattern and silhouette

The Daybreak is a very simple shoe. Its design lines are not complicated. It's the sleek, 70's chic profile that makes the Daybreak a functional and fashionable icon. It is also the feature that counterfeiters do not take the time nor care to replicate.

These two shoes should be the same size! The back height of the fake is 8mm too low. Of course, you can't see this if you don't have the real shoe to compare the height, but you can see why it's low. The fake Nike (right) has a warped and soft heel counter cover. The leather is not glued down properly. The leather counter on the real shoe (left) is smooth and tight.

You can see the dramatically different top line shapes; tall and sleek versus low and humped.

Ⓡ   Ⓕ

Cut and buff outsole side profile

Again, you can see a dramatic difference looking side-on at the heel. First, the shape the white EVA foam is very different. Second, the upper of the fake shoe (right) overhangs the top edge of the white midsole foam.

Notice that the shape of the real midsole (left) is crisp and well defined. We will examine this further coming up.

R

F

The Daybreak heel view

Here you can see what out-of-control shoemaking looks like. The heel padding of the fake (right) is overstuffed, making the heel grossly wide. You can also see that the upper pattern is crooked, the centerline is not centered, and the entire pattern is slanting lower on the lateral side topline. Below, we look inside and see the poorly fit, wrinkled, and twisted footbed.

R

F

The Nike Daybreak lasting construction

The Nike Daybreak midsole is made by the cut and buff process. The midsole outline is cut from a sheet of foam and buffed to create the angled sidewall. The top of the midsole is flat and the shoe upper's edge is lasted under the paper board.

The fake shoe is made with an undersized Stobel sock that pulls the edge of the upper to hide the Strobel stitching. This is why the upper is very loose; it is difficult to get this style of upper tight using the Strobel process.

It is the boarding-lasting process that helps create the Daybreak's sleek profile and narrow waist.

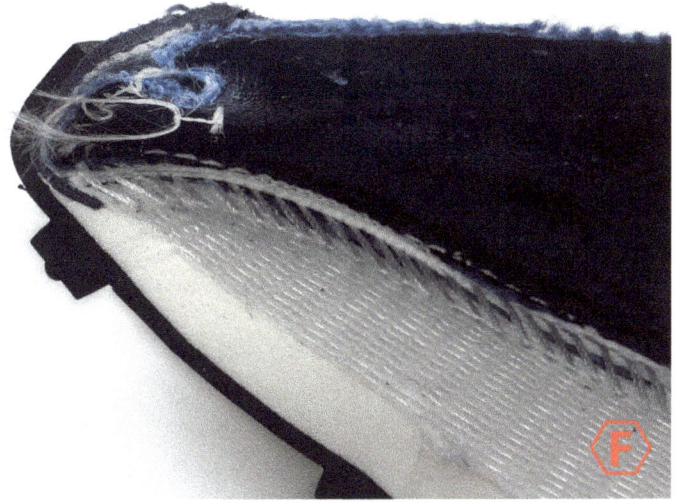

Toe tip construction

Here you can see how far the board-lasting press can pull the upper material together under the shoe. The shoe on the left is correct. You can also see the vamp lining material is color-matched. On the right side, we see the Strobel technique was used. Note the stitching. You can also see the counterfeit factory was not able to pull the vamp pattern tight. See the material bunched up at the toe? This would not be a comfortable shoe to wear.

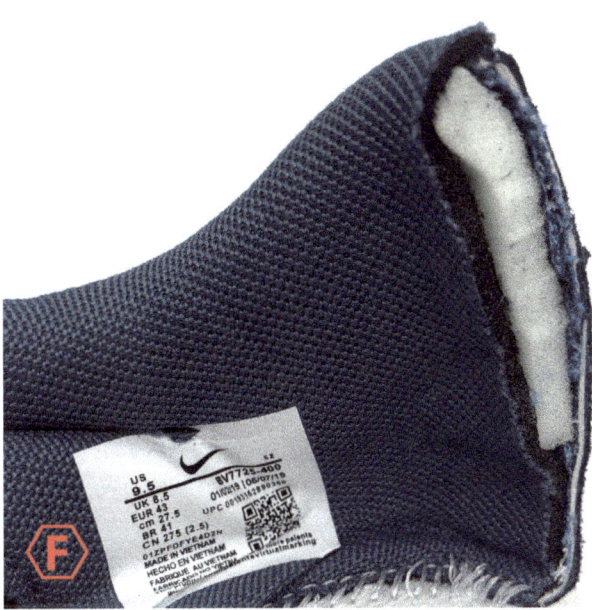

Heel lining pattern

You can see the different lining patterns in these two photos (the fake on the left and the real on the right). The fake shoe has a very conventional solid lining pattern. The real Daybreak has a scalloped pattern with the side panels removed. Also, the fake shoe's collar lining is terribly wrinkled as it wraps to the Strobel sock.

In the cut section of the fake (left), we can see the collar foam is overstuffed, and the heel counter reinforcement layer (glued to the leather heel counter cover) is thin, wrinkled, and cut short.

We can also see the inside size tag is printed on the heel lining. This is not correct. The size tag should be sewn onto the edge of the footbed.

Finally, on top of all these problems, the lining material on the fake is incorrect. The weave is too heavy.

The Daybreak outsole unit

The outsole of the counterfeit Daybreak is much wider than the authentic Nike-made shoe. The fake shoe is made by the Strobel construction method, thus the factory made the size larger to cover the perimeter Strobel stitch. The real Nike shoe is board-lasted, allowing the waist to be cut in. There is no stitching to hide.

Interesting secrets hidden inside

These shoes both have interesting secrets hidden inside. As we have seen, the fake (on the left below) is made by the Strobel process. This is incorrect for this shoe type. Yet, when we peel up the white woven Strobel sock, we can see the die-cut size marking. The EVA wedge midsole on the fake is made using the correct cut and buff process.

When we peel up the brown paper lasting board of the authentic Nike-made Daybreak, we see the top of the midsole wedge has modeled flex grooves and raised letters. Nike has updated the manufacturing method on this shoe to the more efficient molded EVA instead of the old-fashioned, wasteful, cut and buff process.

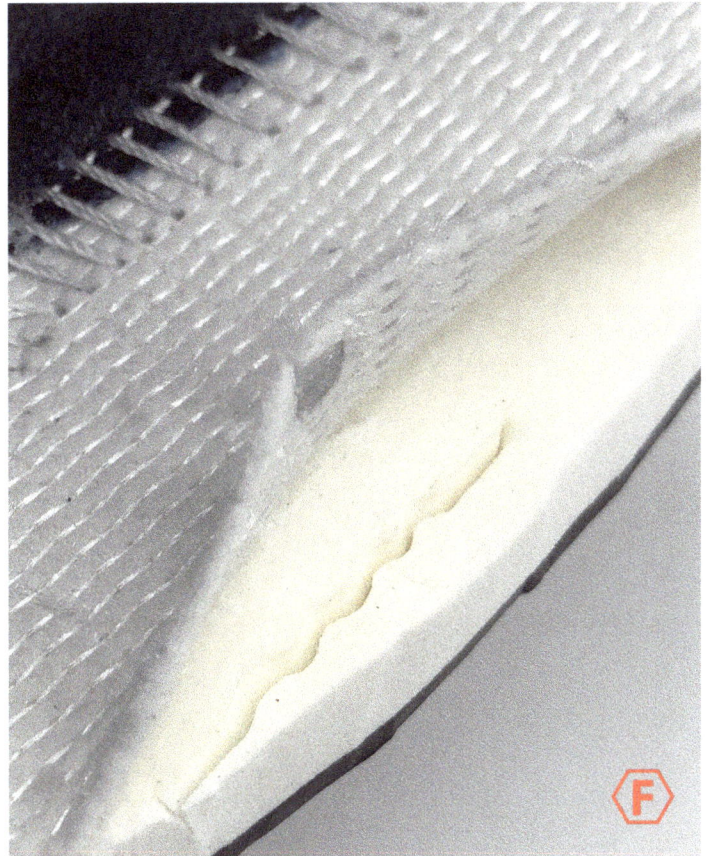

Outsole logo

We can see the outsole logo of the fake Daybreak has some major problems. The logo lettering is not complete. Either the logo tooling was not cut correctly or the tooling was damaged. The counterfeit rubber pressing factory most likely did not take time to clean and maintain the pressing equipment. Air bubbles and heavy texture are also often found on low quality fakes.

The Authentic Nike Daybreak

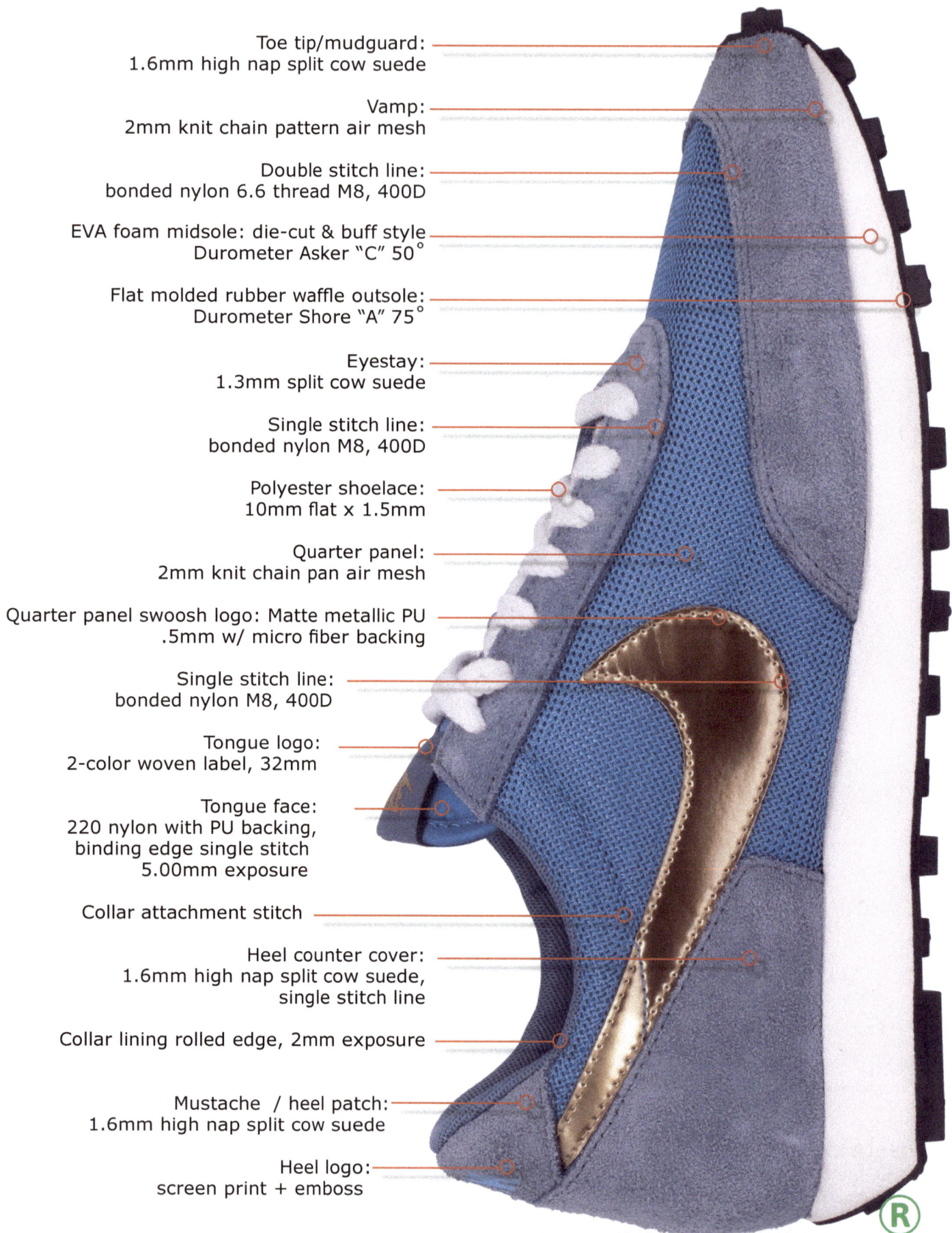

Toe tip/mudguard:
1.6mm high nap split cow suede

Vamp:
2mm knit chain pattern air mesh

Double stitch line:
bonded nylon 6.6 thread M8, 400D

EVA foam midsole: die-cut & buff style
Durometer Asker "C" 50°

Flat molded rubber waffle outsole:
Durometer Shore "A" 75°

Eyestay:
1.3mm split cow suede

Single stitch line:
bonded nylon M8, 400D

Polyester shoelace:
10mm flat x 1.5mm

Quarter panel:
2mm knit chain pan air mesh

Quarter panel swoosh logo: Matte metallic PU
.5mm w/ micro fiber backing

Single stitch line:
bonded nylon M8, 400D

Tongue logo:
2-color woven label, 32mm

Tongue face:
220 nylon with PU backing,
binding edge single stitch
5.00mm exposure

Collar attachment stitch

Heel counter cover:
1.6mm high nap split cow suede,
single stitch line

Collar lining rolled edge, 2mm exposure

Mustache / heel patch:
1.6mm high nap split cow suede

Heel logo:
screen print + emboss

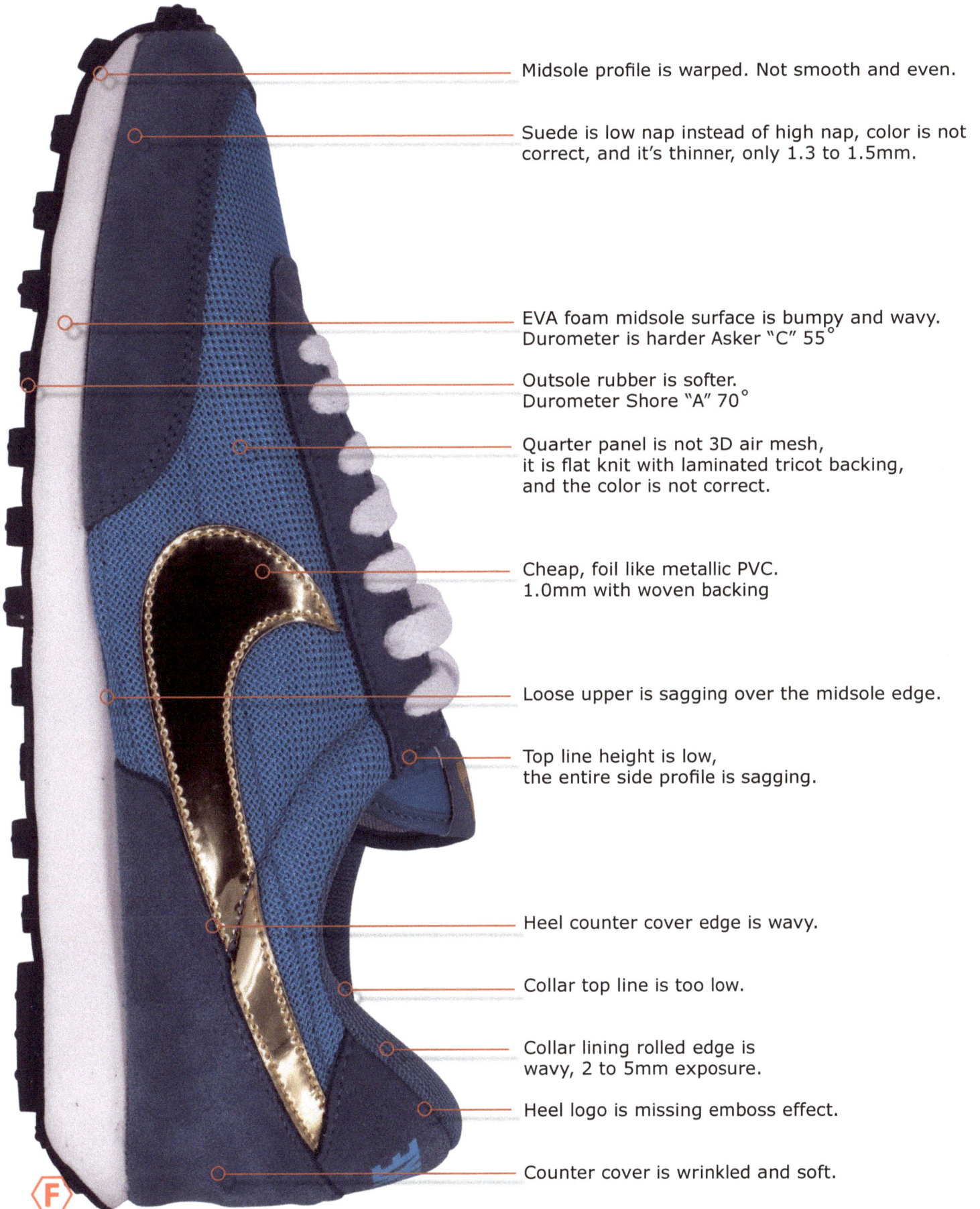

Midsole profile is warped. Not smooth and even.

Suede is low nap instead of high nap, color is not correct, and it's thinner, only 1.3 to 1.5mm.

EVA foam midsole surface is bumpy and wavy. Durometer is harder Asker "C" 55°

Outsole rubber is softer. Durometer Shore "A" 70°

Quarter panel is not 3D air mesh, it is flat knit with laminated tricot backing, and the color is not correct.

Cheap, foil like metallic PVC. 1.0mm with woven backing

Loose upper is sagging over the midsole edge.

Top line height is low, the entire side profile is sagging.

Heel counter cover edge is wavy.

Collar top line is too low.

Collar lining rolled edge is wavy, 2 to 5mm exposure.

Heel logo is missing emboss effect.

Counter cover is wrinkled and soft.

F

Inside the real Nike Daybreak

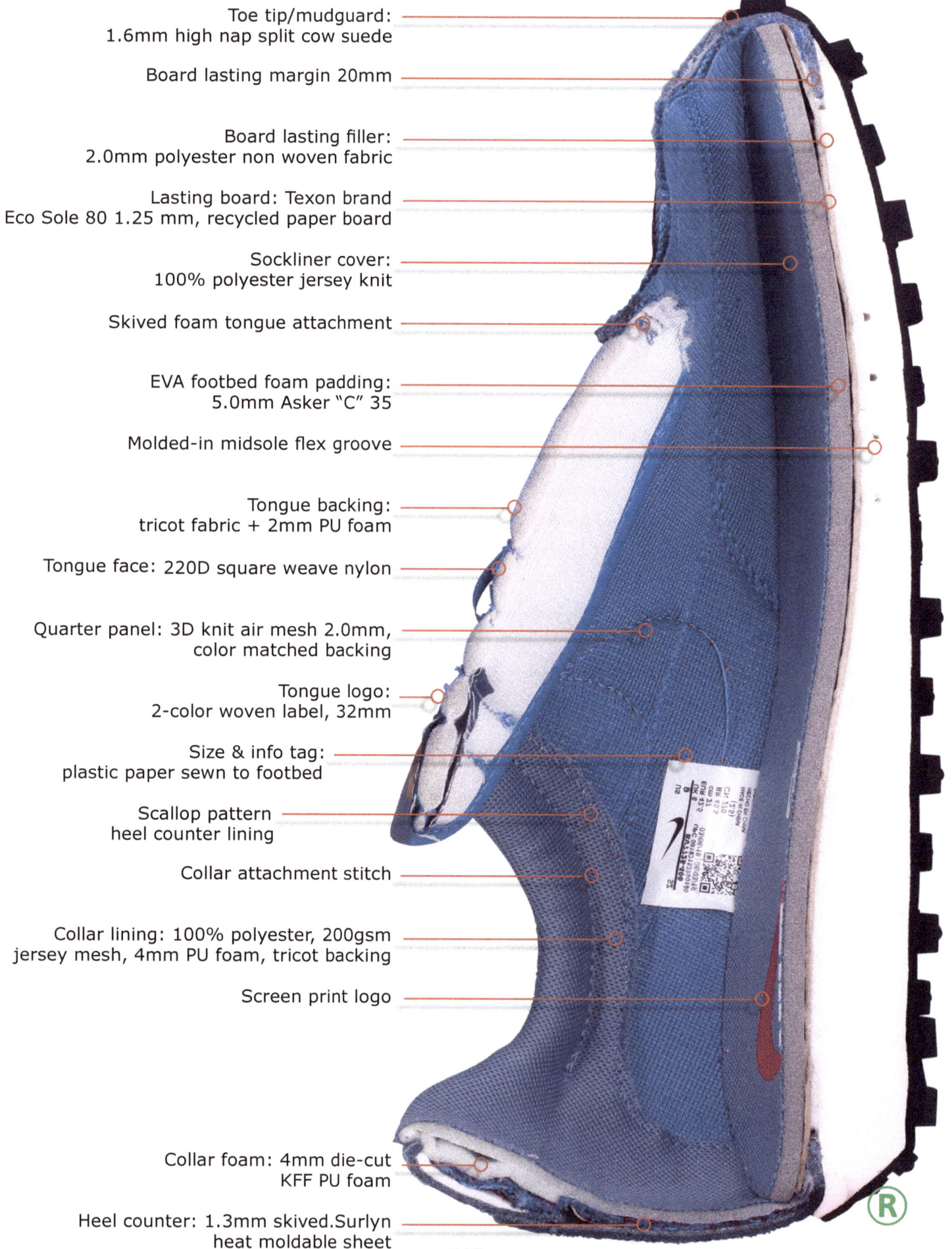

Toe tip/mudguard:
1.6mm high nap split cow suede

Board lasting margin 20mm

Board lasting filler:
2.0mm polyester non woven fabric

Lasting board: Texon brand
Eco Sole 80 1.25 mm, recycled paper board

Sockliner cover:
100% polyester jersey knit

Skived foam tongue attachment

EVA footbed foam padding:
5.0mm Asker "C" 35

Molded-in midsole flex groove

Tongue backing:
tricot fabric + 2mm PU foam

Tongue face: 220D square weave nylon

Quarter panel: 3D knit air mesh 2.0mm,
color matched backing

Tongue logo:
2-color woven label, 32mm

Size & info tag:
plastic paper sewn to footbed

Scallop pattern
heel counter lining

Collar attachment stitch

Collar lining: 100% polyester, 200gsm
jersey mesh, 4mm PU foam, tricot backing

Screen print logo

Collar foam: 4mm die-cut
KFF PU foam

Heel counter: 1.3mm skived.Surlyn
heat moldable sheet

Inside the fake Nike Daybreak

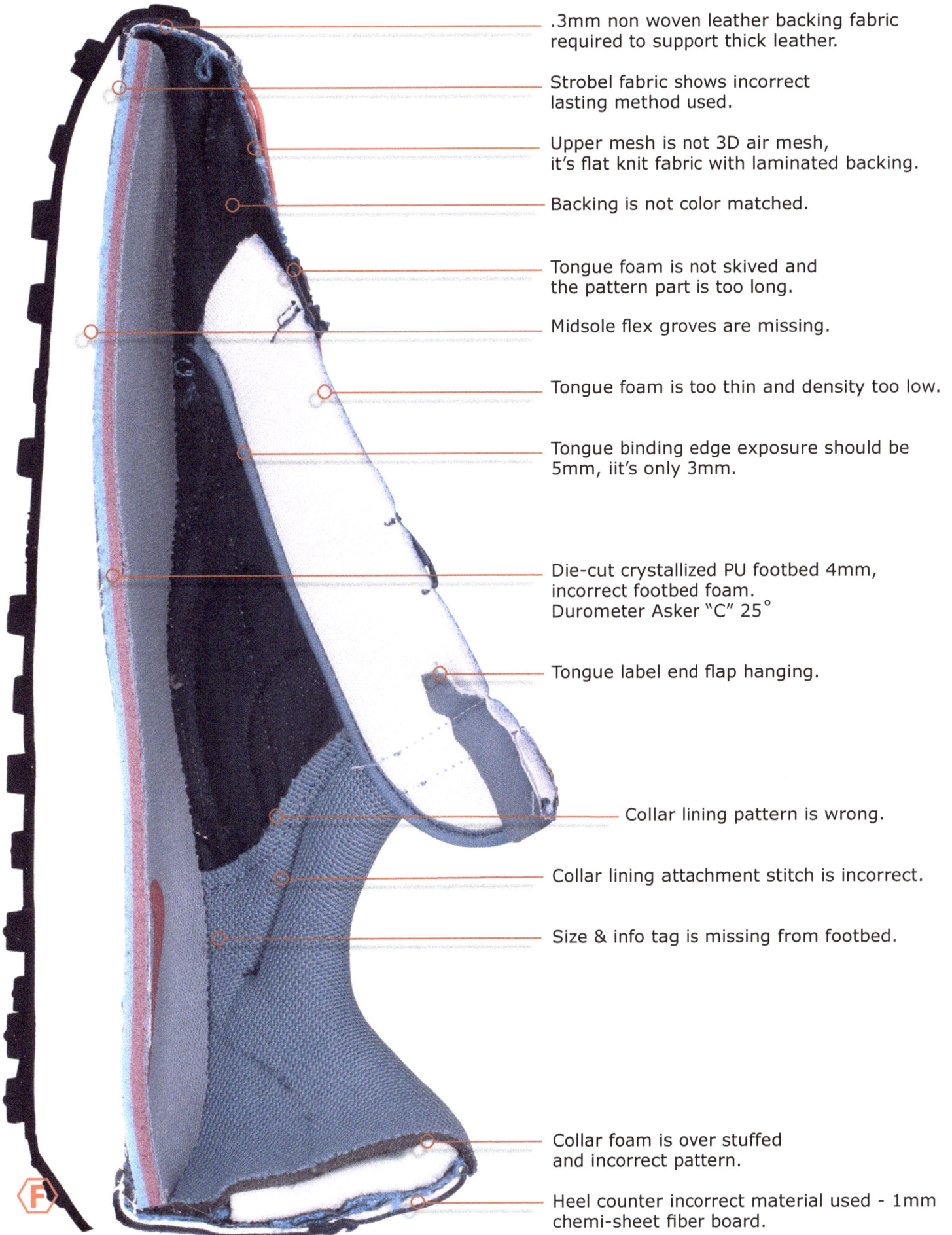

.3mm non woven leather backing fabric required to support thick leather.

Strobel fabric shows incorrect lasting method used.

Upper mesh is not 3D air mesh, it's flat knit fabric with laminated backing.

Backing is not color matched.

Tongue foam is not skived and the pattern part is too long.

Midsole flex groves are missing.

Tongue foam is too thin and density too low.

Tongue binding edge exposure should be 5mm, iit's only 3mm.

Die-cut crystallized PU footbed 4mm, incorrect footbed foam.
Durometer Asker "C" 25°

Tongue label end flap hanging.

Collar lining pattern is wrong.

Collar lining attachment stitch is incorrect.

Size & info tag is missing from footbed.

Collar foam is over stuffed and incorrect pattern.

Heel counter incorrect material used - 1mm chemi-sheet fiber board.

F

Chapter 12 : How to Spot a Fake Adidas Yeezy 500

Spotting a fake Adidas Yeezy 500

The Yeezy 500 is an Adidas shoe designed by the famous rap star Kanye West. West is one of the world's best-selling music artists, with more than 160 million records sold worldwide. Kanye West has been an outspoken and very controversial celebrity throughout his career.

Propelled the singer's megastar status, the Yeezy brand surged in popularity. In 2020, the Yeezy brand reached sales of $1.5 billion. This sales success has put the Jordan brand team on notice. With sales of just over $3.0 billion, Nike has a real challenger.

The Yeezy brand's rapid rise and sky-high prices have made the brand an obvious target for counterfeiters. The Yeezy 500's lack of exotic and expensive technology makes it an inviting prospect for replication.

Product provenance

In this chapter, we have two different pairs of the Yeezy 500 that we cut-up and analyzed in-depth. We will study an authentic Yeezy 500 purchased directly from StockX and its counterfeit shoe imported from South China.

Authenticating the Adidas Yeezy 500
What to look for

Kanye will be angry when he sees this.
The first things to look at when comparing the fake and the real Yeezy 500s are the materials and the workmanship.

While looking at the Yeezy materials, also study the build. Adidas's real Yeezy is not built to perfection, but the counterfeit Yeezy is clearly not made to the same quality standards.

Color matching is difficult for monotone shoes made with many different materials.

Check the material; the leather quality for premium products must be top notch.

Adidas builds top quality tooling. Gaps, air vents, and wrinkles are not acceptable.

The Yeezy 500 has many material edges; make sure they are cleanly cut.

The Yeezy 500 tongue is complicated and difficult to make cleanly. Look for wrinkles.

Does the 3M reflective tape really reflect?

Check the side profile, the Yeezy 500 is unique and easy to mess up.

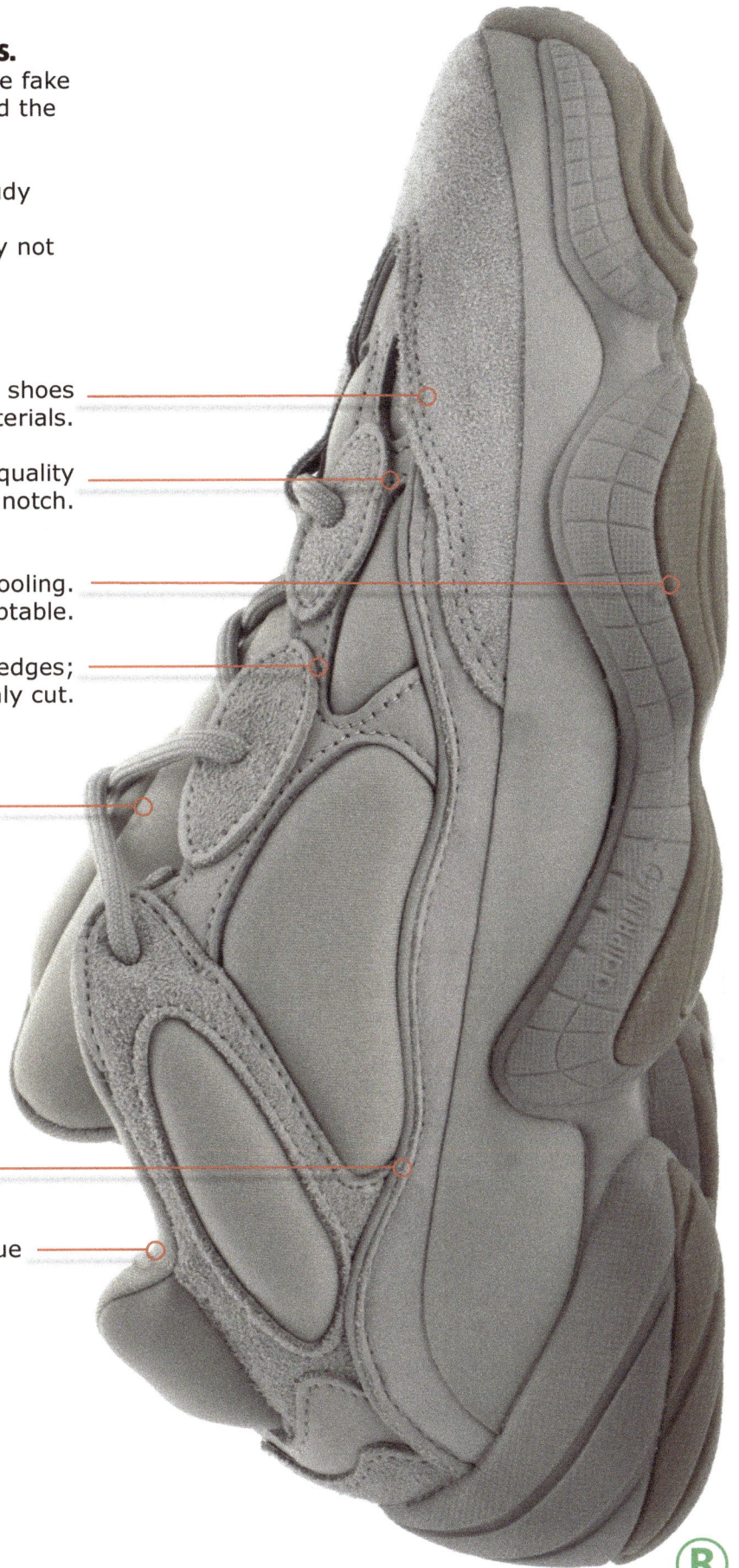

What is the real Yeezy 500 made of?

The real Kanye West designed Yeezy 500 is made with a mix of genuine suede, nubuck, and pigmented full-grain leather. The suede is medium nap, so it is always a bit hairy.

To clean up the hairy edges, Adidas has color-embossed the edges. You can see this on the eye stay parts as well as the ankle strap. The eye-stay underlay is a pigmented full-grain leather. The surface is uniform in color with a slight texture emboss. You can see it's genuine leather by the texture of the cut edge.

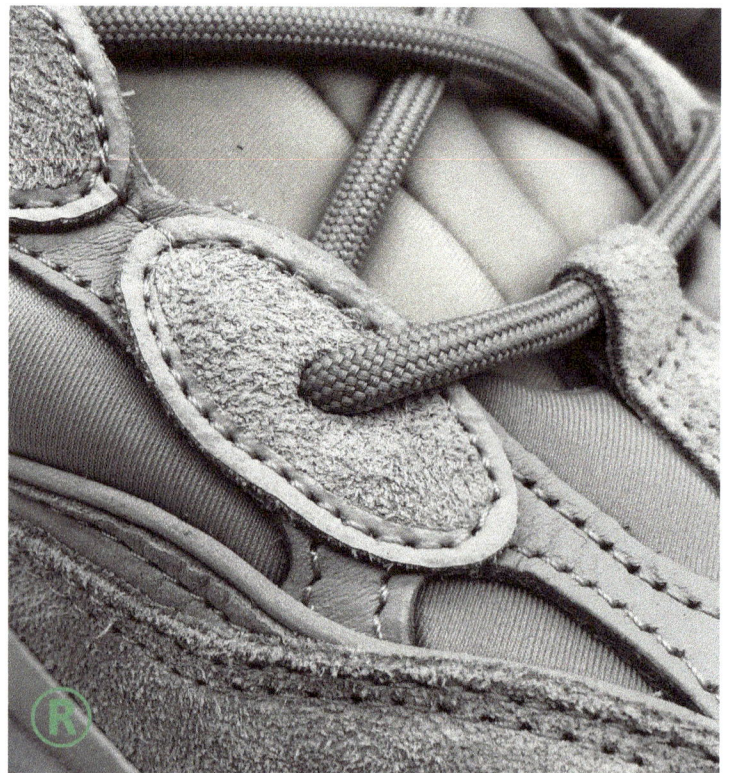

The Adidas Yeezy 500 is not an easy shoe to produce. It does not feature any special technology, unique material, or process, but its overall design is challenging to assembe neatly. The small suede eyestay parts with their die-cut edges are difficult to make clean. In an attempt to clean up the cut edge of the suede parts, Adidas screen printed around the edges. This effect is marginally successful; for some reason, they let the collar panel go ragged.

This shoe is a study of how to handle cut edges. The Yeezy 500 is a jumble of clean, smooth, lumpy, jagged, and ragged edges.

Our fake Yeezy 500 is constructed with low-quality, high-nap belly suede. The surface is rough and hairy. You can also feel the leather's substance is soft and spongy, not the firm high-quality suede of the real Adidas-made Yeezy. The eyestay underlay is synthetic PU with a leather-like embossed surface.

(F)

On the real Yeezy, the rubber foxing overlays a panel of brushed nubuck leather. This high-quality nubuck leather has a smooth, uniform, and velvety surface.

(R)

Cut materials edges

If you look at the edges, you see the synthetic backing fiber is grey-blue. This is not the same leather as the original Yeezy 500. The fake Yeezy has swapped PU nubuck for the genuine nubuck leather on the real rubber underlay panel. The plastic-looking surface and white backing edge are dead giveaways that this shoe is fake.

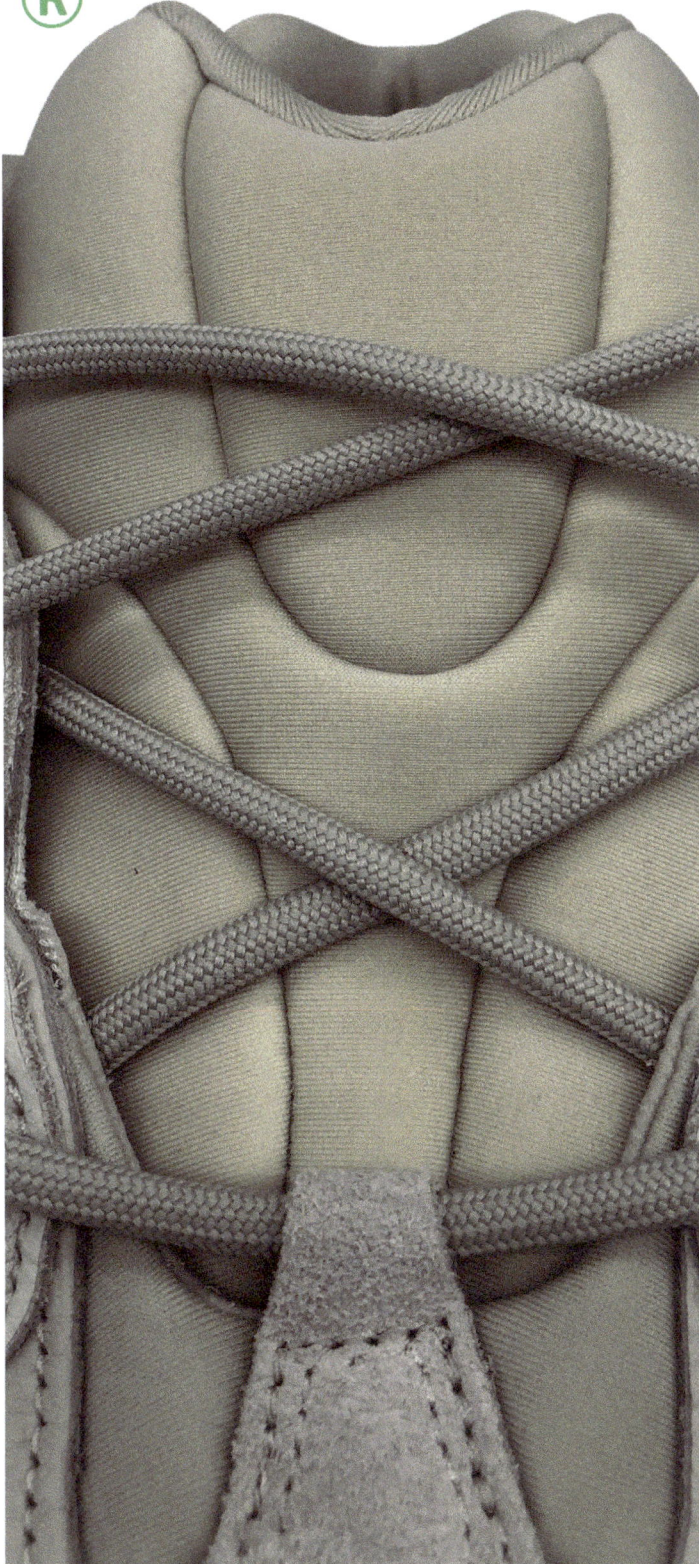

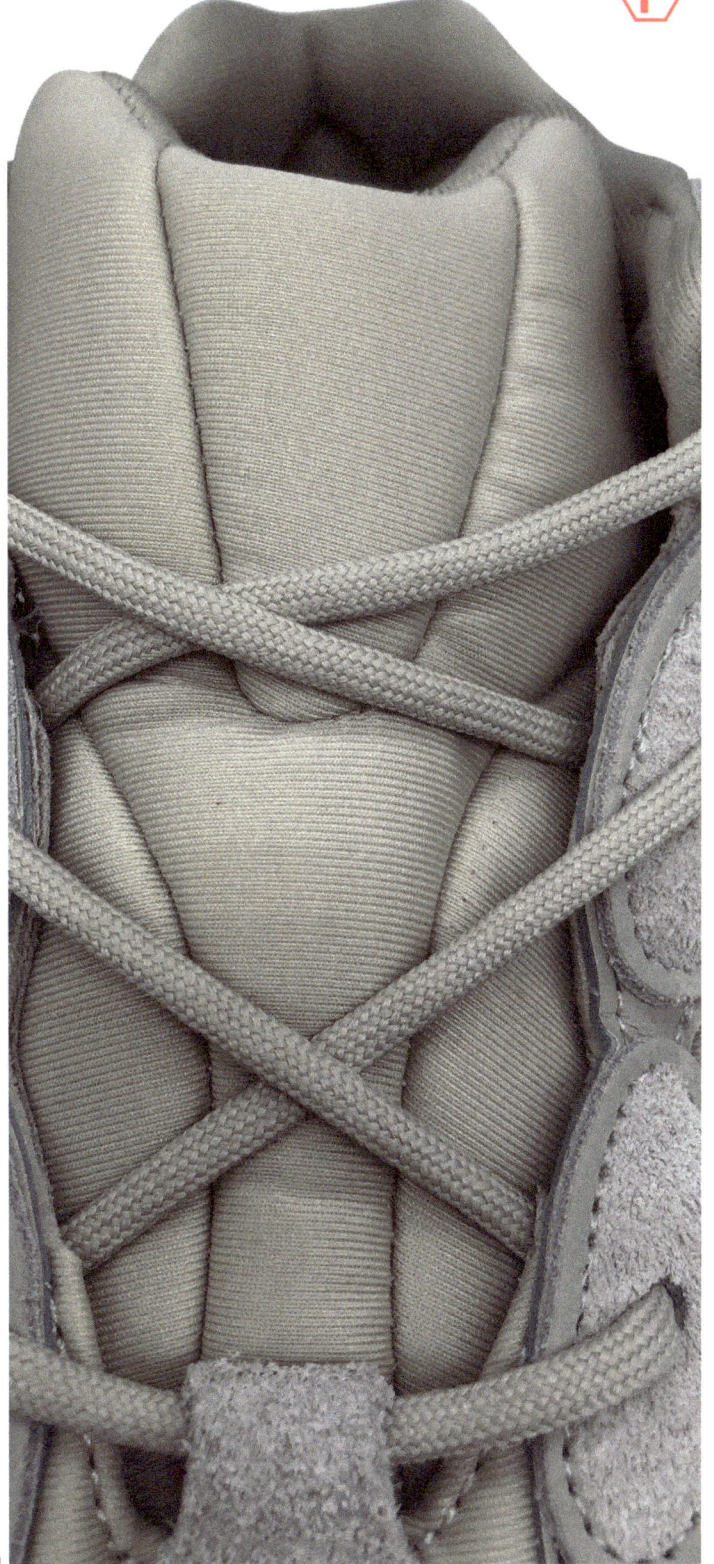

The Yeezy 500 tongue

Looking at the tongue face of our two Yeezys, you can see dramatic differences in material quality and workmanship. The real Yeezy 500 tongue has smooth contours made with a firm foam wrinkle-free fabric. The fake tongue shows open seams, wrinkled fabric, and soft creased foam backing.

Also, look at the base of the tongue. The real Yeezy 500 has a smooth rolled edge with a reversed seam. The fake has a rolled edge and needs extra stitching to hold the material flat.

The Yeezy pattern and silhouette

Kanye West's Yeezy 500 pattern is a complicated collection of curves, overlays, and contrasting material underlays. It is a challenging shoe to make and very difficult to copy. Side-by-side, you can see the crisp silhouette lines on the real shoe (left) versus the copy shoe. Notice how the instep contour and collar top line of the original are well defined.

On the heel view, you can clearly see the fake pattern has missed the mark.

125

The Yeezy 500 outsole unit

Adidas has dusted off the 90's vintage "feet you wear" technology for the Yeezy 500 outsole design. The 500 is a unique and patented pattern of foot pods and midsole structures. The fake outsole unit is nearly identical. The tooling design for the rubber compression outsole is well duplicated. However, the color of the rubber is not correct, and the compound is slightly softer than the authentic.

We zoomed in on the toe tip to get a good look at the Adidas "mountain" logo. The fake Adidas logo is well made in this case but not in all cases.

The EVA midsole of the counterfeit Yeezy 500 is close but just not made to the same quality standard. The fake midsole has some pigment issues and some extra air vents you don't see on the authentic Adidas sneaker. We zoomed in on the side logo here. You can see extra air vents on the logo and venting on the midsole edge.

126

Inside the cut open Yeezy 500

First off, you can see the fake Yeezy 500 (right) is missing the injection-molded shank. You don't have to cut your shoes open to check this feature; you can remove the footbed and press on the Strobel bottom with your fingers— you can feel the end of the shank.

Inside the tongue

The tongue section clearly shows how the real Yeezy internals are neatly assembled while the fake Yeezy tongue is a mess of layers and bunched-up foam parts.

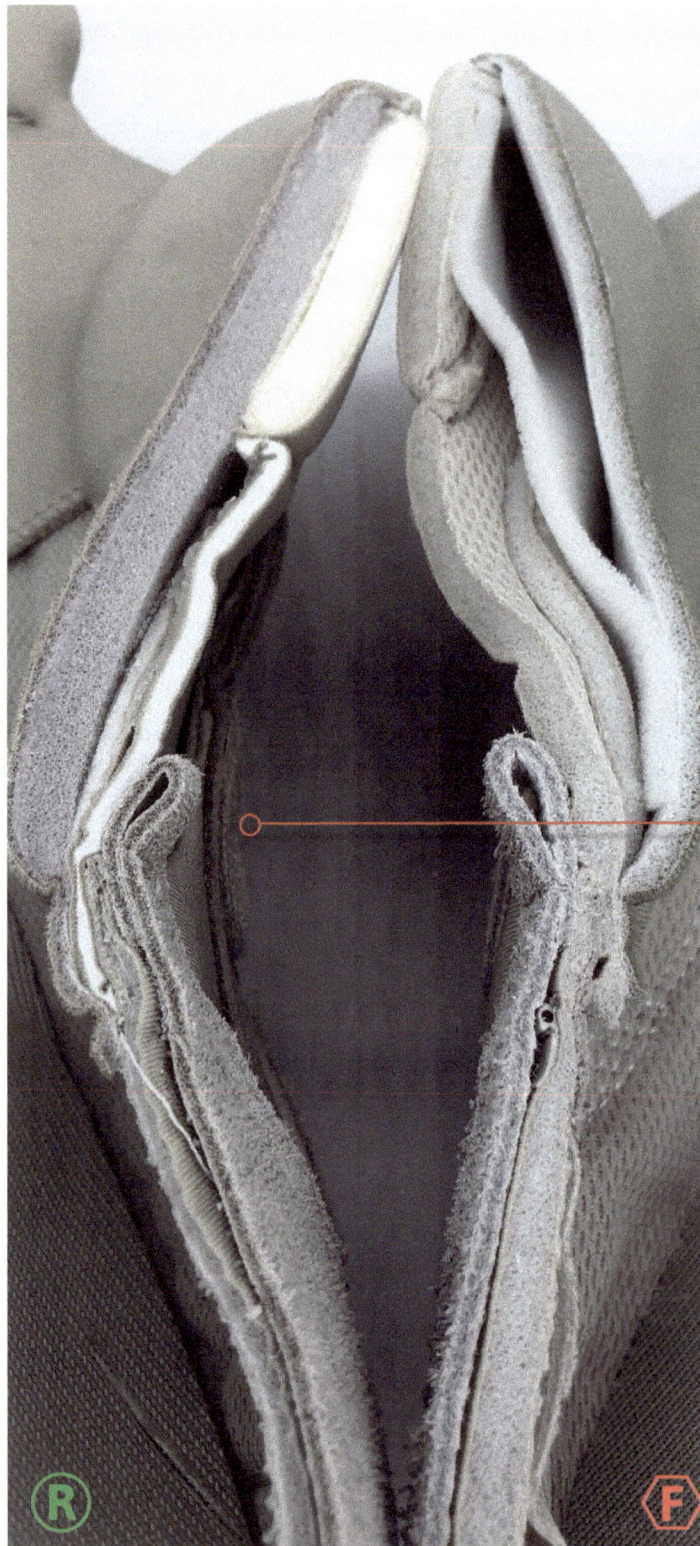

127

The Yeezy 500 internal construction

The cross-section of the heel shows you just how poorly the fake (left) shoe is made. You can see the internal layers of the fake are not bonded together. Air gaps and voids will wrinkle as the shoe is worn.

The collar foam of the authentic Yeezy is segmented and well shaped and stops short of the heel pocket. The collar foam of the counterfeit Yeezy runs too deep and stops just short of the footbed edge.

The authentic Adidas-made Yeezy (right) has a thick injection molded heel counter made of sturdy plastic. The heel counter of fake is paper thin and will not provide support.

F

R

128

The Yeezy 500 vamp lining construction

The cross-section of the vamp shows a critical construction shortcut. In the real shoe (left), you can see the vamp lining is smooth with no stitching. This lining is "hung" inside the shoe.

The lining of the counterfeit shoe is crisscrossed with stitches from the outside of the shoe. To speed up the production of the fake, the factory combined the upper and lining parts and stitched the components together in a single speedy operation.
This is efficient but at the expense of comfort.

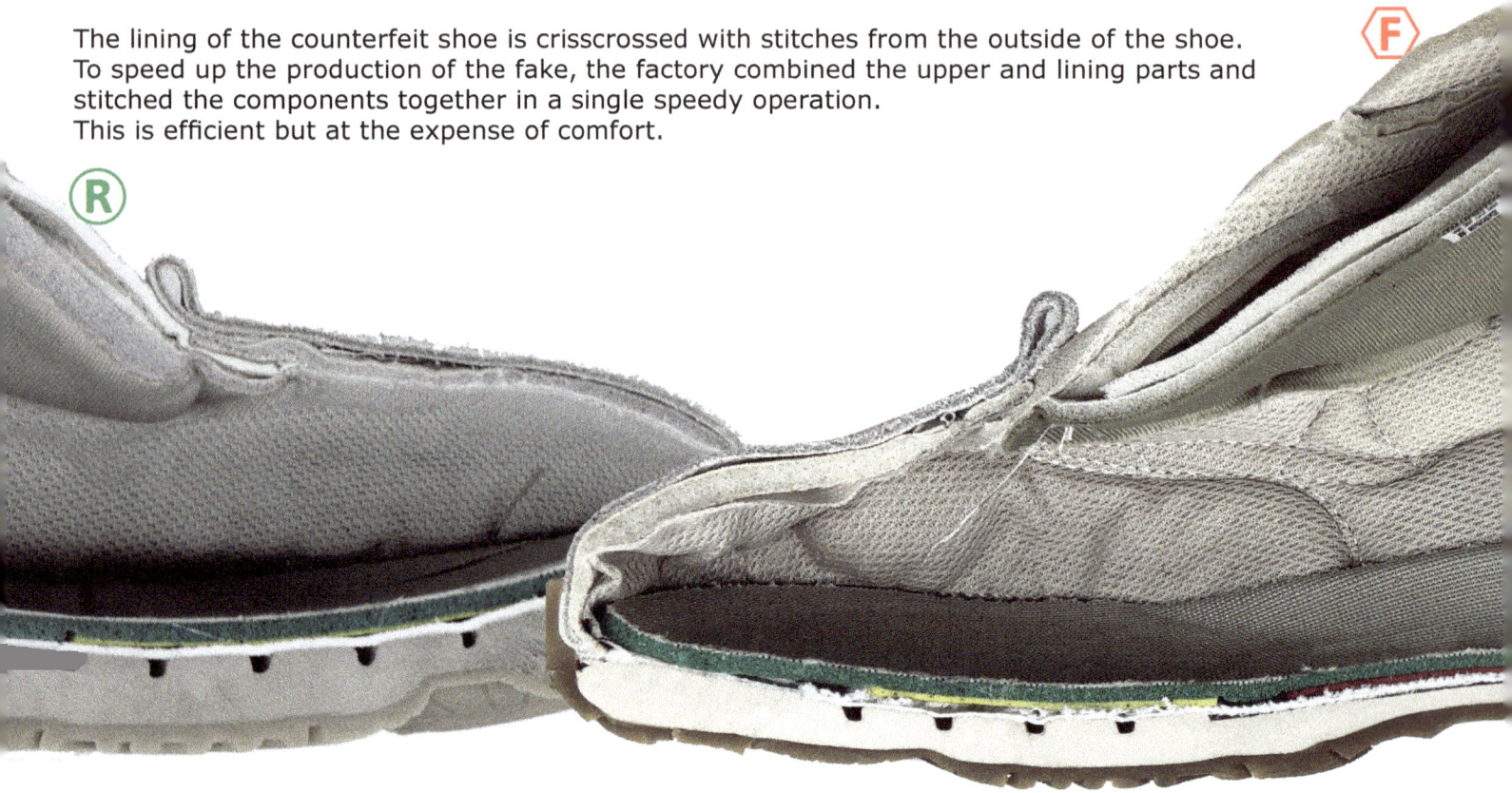

The Yeezy footbed

Interestingly, the counterfeit Yeezy has a softer footbed. Normally, you would expect the fake to be very stiff with cardboard-like foam. Both the authentic and counterfeit are marked with the Ortholite trademark, but you can see the color inserts are not correctly placed on the fake Yeezy footbed.

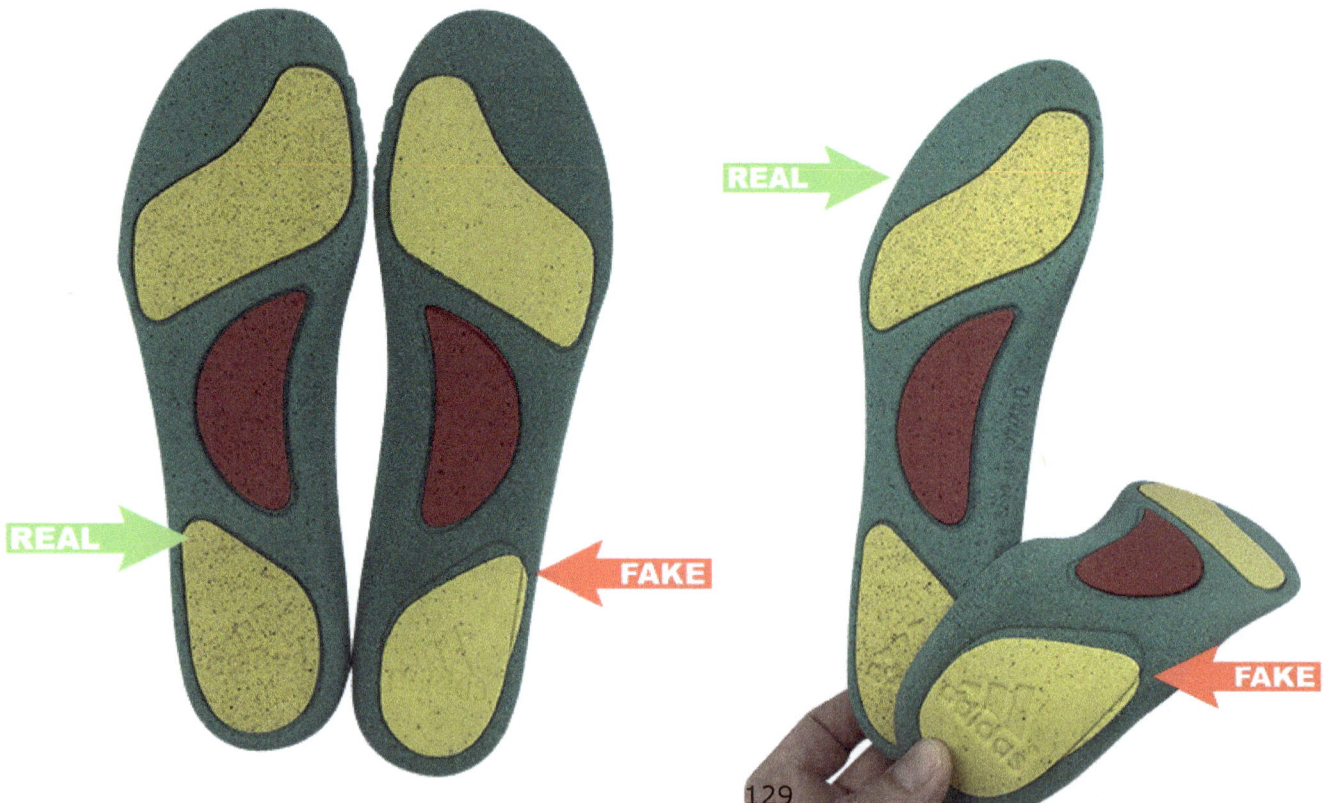

129

(R)

(F)

Overall

After looking at the upper materials, outsole parts, and internal construction, we can see this is an counterfeit Adidas Yeezy 500. This fake shoe (right) suffers from the common faults: poor shoemaking and low spec material substitutions.

Does the fake look like a Yeezy 500? Mostly. Will the fake Yeezy be comfortable to wear and long-lasting? No. This fake is a poorly made pile of junk that damages the Adidas brand as well as your feet.

The Authentic Adidas Yeezy 500

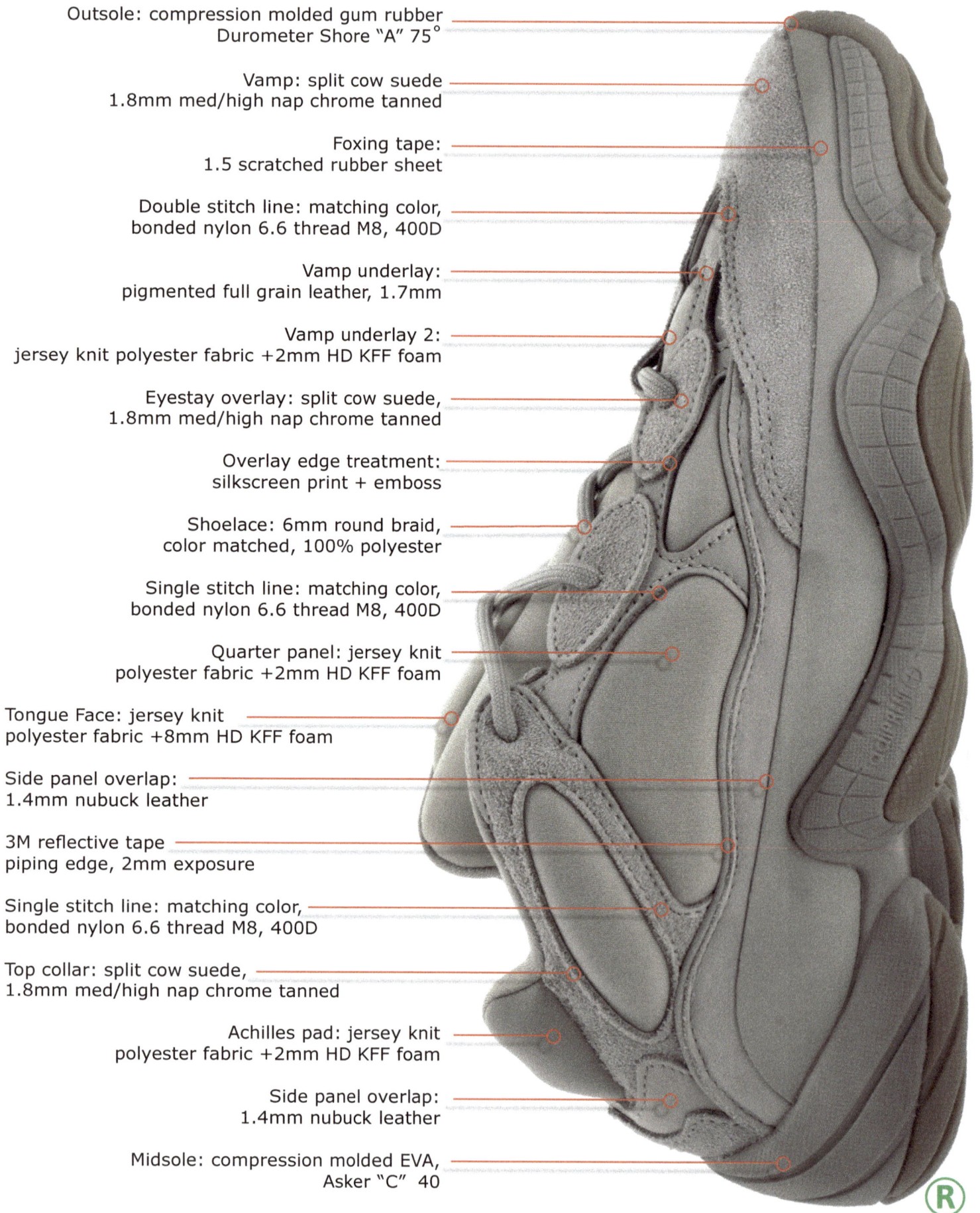

Outsole: compression molded gum rubber
Durometer Shore "A" 75°

Vamp: split cow suede
1.8mm med/high nap chrome tanned

Foxing tape:
1.5 scratched rubber sheet

Double stitch line: matching color,
bonded nylon 6.6 thread M8, 400D

Vamp underlay:
pigmented full grain leather, 1.7mm

Vamp underlay 2:
jersey knit polyester fabric +2mm HD KFF foam

Eyestay overlay: split cow suede,
1.8mm med/high nap chrome tanned

Overlay edge treatment:
silkscreen print + emboss

Shoelace: 6mm round braid,
color matched, 100% polyester

Single stitch line: matching color,
bonded nylon 6.6 thread M8, 400D

Quarter panel: jersey knit
polyester fabric +2mm HD KFF foam

Tongue Face: jersey knit
polyester fabric +8mm HD KFF foam

Side panel overlap:
1.4mm nubuck leather

3M reflective tape
piping edge, 2mm exposure

Single stitch line: matching color,
bonded nylon 6.6 thread M8, 400D

Top collar: split cow suede,
1.8mm med/high nap chrome tanned

Achilles pad: jersey knit
polyester fabric +2mm HD KFF foam

Side panel overlap:
1.4mm nubuck leather

Midsole: compression molded EVA,
Asker "C" 40

®

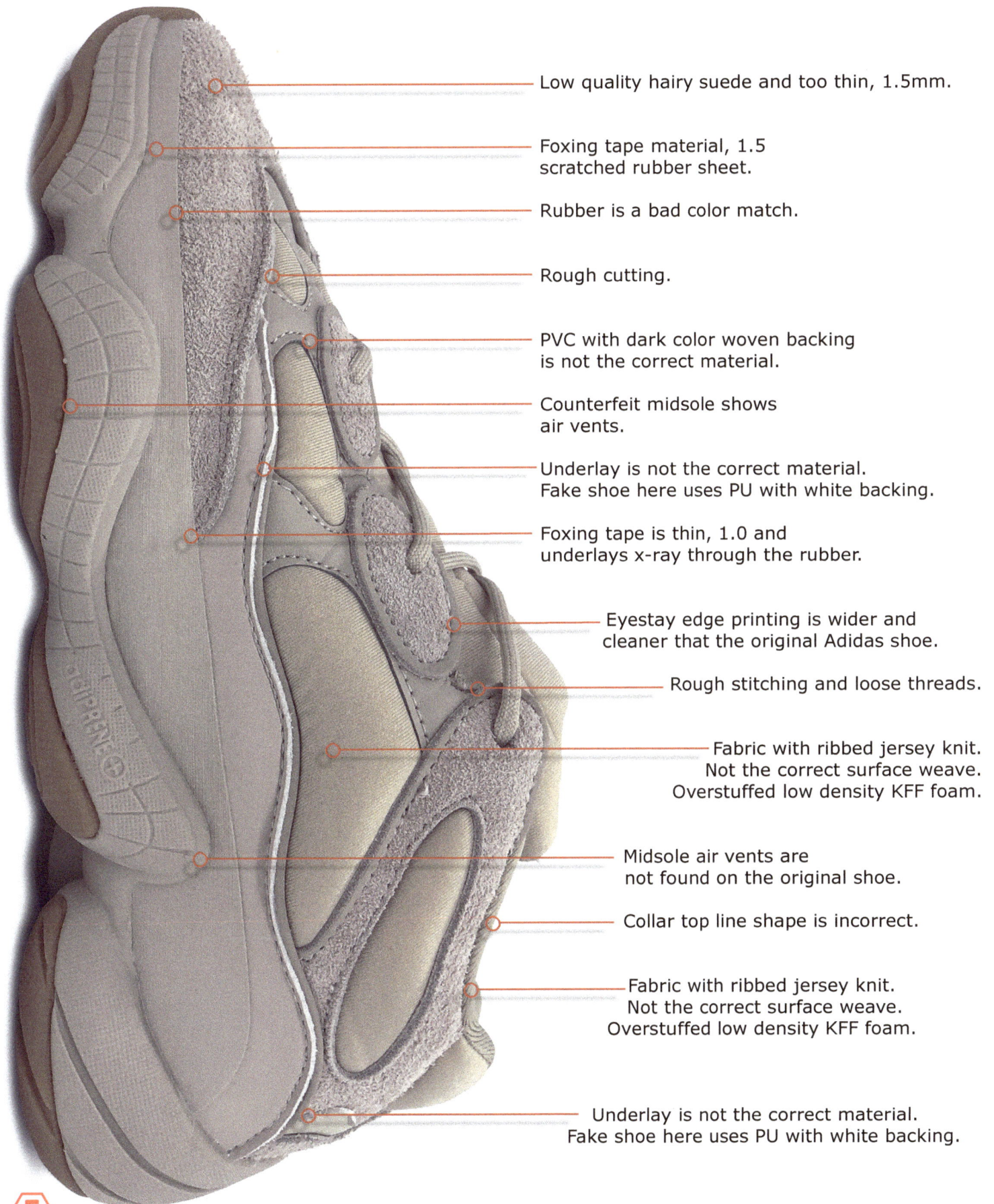

Low quality hairy suede and too thin, 1.5mm.

Foxing tape material, 1.5 scratched rubber sheet.

Rubber is a bad color match.

Rough cutting.

PVC with dark color woven backing is not the correct material.

Counterfeit midsole shows air vents.

Underlay is not the correct material. Fake shoe here uses PU with white backing.

Foxing tape is thin, 1.0 and underlays x-ray through the rubber.

Eyestay edge printing is wider and cleaner that the original Adidas shoe.

Rough stitching and loose threads.

Fabric with ribbed jersey knit. Not the correct surface weave. Overstuffed low density KFF foam.

Midsole air vents are not found on the original shoe.

Collar top line shape is incorrect.

Fabric with ribbed jersey knit. Not the correct surface weave. Overstuffed low density KFF foam.

Underlay is not the correct material. Fake shoe here uses PU with white backing.

F

Inside The Authentic Adidas Yeezy 500

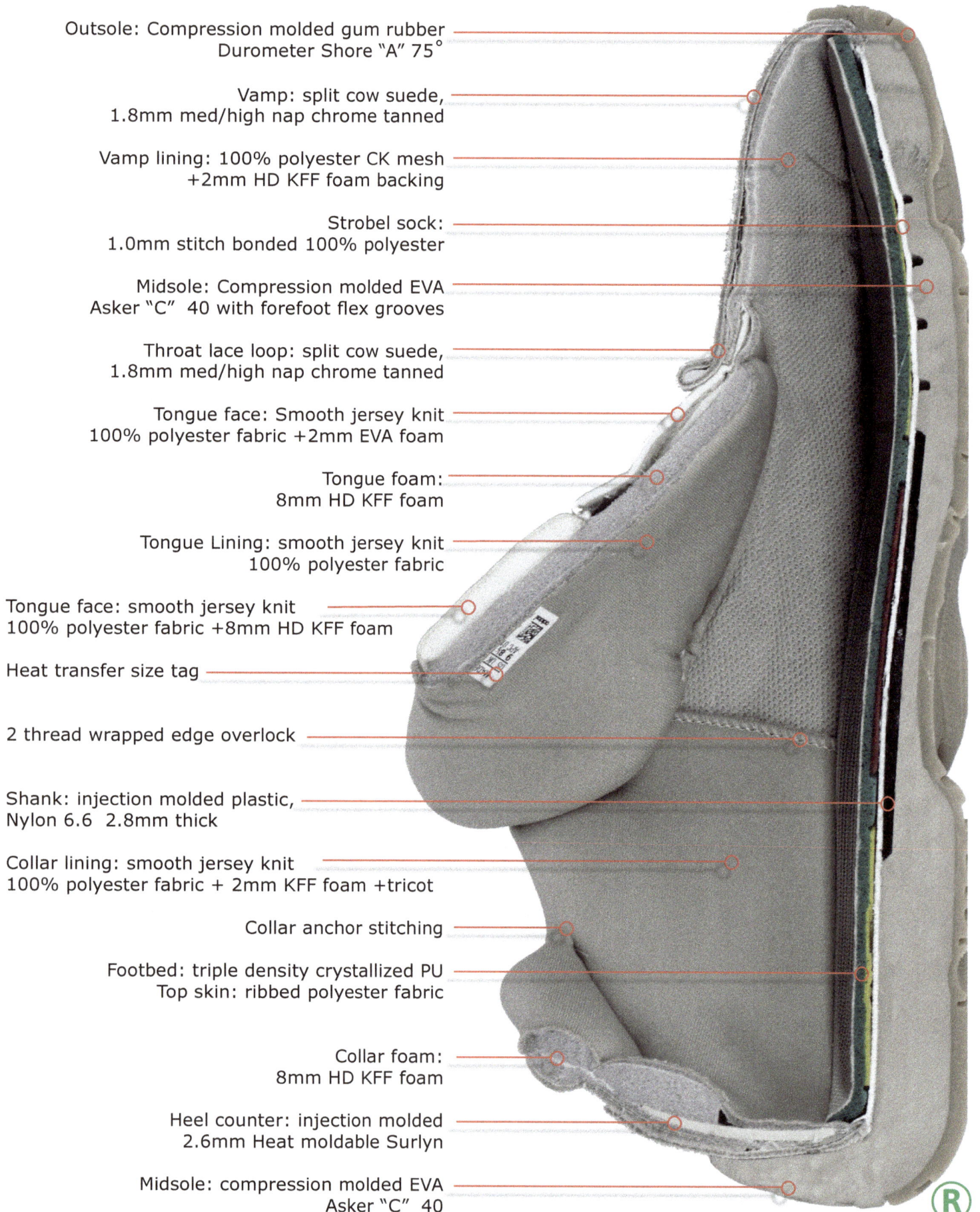

Outsole: Compression molded gum rubber
Durometer Shore "A" 75°

Vamp: split cow suede,
1.8mm med/high nap chrome tanned

Vamp lining: 100% polyester CK mesh
+2mm HD KFF foam backing

Strobel sock:
1.0mm stitch bonded 100% polyester

Midsole: Compression molded EVA
Asker "C" 40 with forefoot flex grooves

Throat lace loop: split cow suede,
1.8mm med/high nap chrome tanned

Tongue face: Smooth jersey knit
100% polyester fabric +2mm EVA foam

Tongue foam:
8mm HD KFF foam

Tongue Lining: smooth jersey knit
100% polyester fabric

Tongue face: smooth jersey knit
100% polyester fabric +8mm HD KFF foam

Heat transfer size tag

2 thread wrapped edge overlock

Shank: injection molded plastic,
Nylon 6.6 2.8mm thick

Collar lining: smooth jersey knit
100% polyester fabric + 2mm KFF foam +tricot

Collar anchor stitching

Footbed: triple density crystallized PU
Top skin: ribbed polyester fabric

Collar foam:
8mm HD KFF foam

Heel counter: injection molded
2.6mm Heat moldable Surlyn

Midsole: compression molded EVA
Asker "C" 40

Ⓡ

133

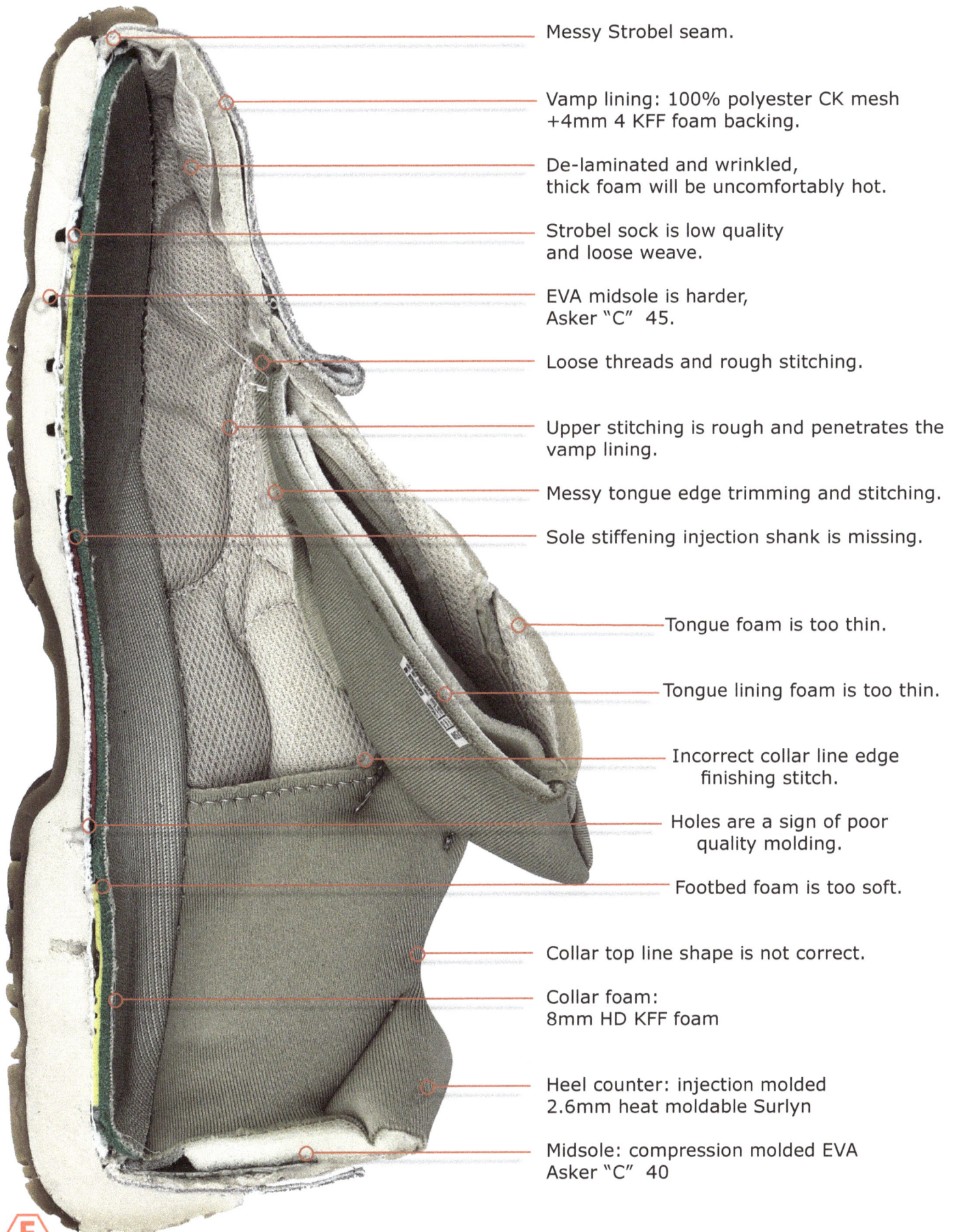

Messy Strobel seam.

Vamp lining: 100% polyester CK mesh +4mm 4 KFF foam backing.

De-laminated and wrinkled, thick foam will be uncomfortably hot.

Strobel sock is low quality and loose weave.

EVA midsole is harder, Asker "C" 45.

Loose threads and rough stitching.

Upper stitching is rough and penetrates the vamp lining.

Messy tongue edge trimming and stitching.

Sole stiffening injection shank is missing.

Tongue foam is too thin.

Tongue lining foam is too thin.

Incorrect collar line edge finishing stitch.

Holes are a sign of poor quality molding.

Footbed foam is too soft.

Collar top line shape is not correct.

Collar foam: 8mm HD KFF foam

Heel counter: injection molded 2.6mm heat moldable Surlyn

Midsole: compression molded EVA Asker "C" 40

F

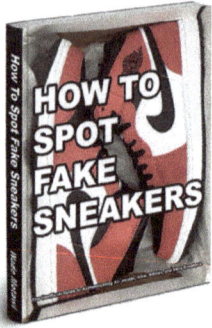

#1 *How to Spot Fake Sneakers*
You will never look at shoes the same way again.
See your favorite Nike, Vans, and Adidas shoes in a whole new way. Our guide to sneaker authentication literately cuts deep into the world of counterfeit sneakers. You will learn how to inspect and authenticate sneakers like a professional. You will speak the language of sneakers and you'll never get burned buying fakes again.

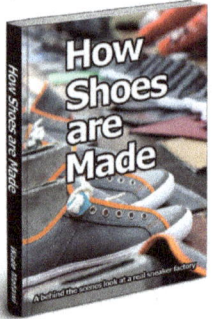

#2 *How Shoes are Made*
Launch your professional shoe career here.
Is your career goal to work for a big brand like Nike or Converse? Maybe you have your own brand and designs to produce and sell? You are in the right place. *How Shoes are Made* is your launching pad - see and learn every step from shoe design to development, manufacturing to exporting, and more from inside a shoe factory.

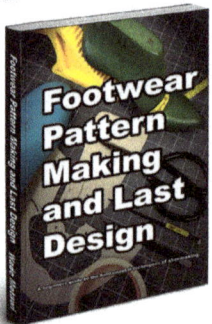

#3 *Footwear Pattern Making and Last Design*
Transform your designs into real shoes.
When you are ready to explore the heart of shoemaking you must understand how the last and pattern work together to create shoe. This book will pull you into the shoemakers world of last design, size grading, and pattern cutting.

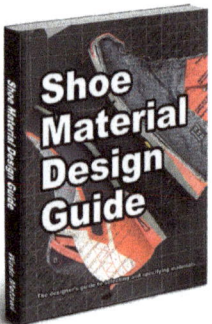

#4 *The Shoe Material Design Guide*
Materials make it real
Turn your drawings into factory ready footwear specifications. You will learn how to specify a shoe by looking inside the classic styles of modern footwear. This book shows you what materials Nike and Adidas pick to build their iconic shoes.

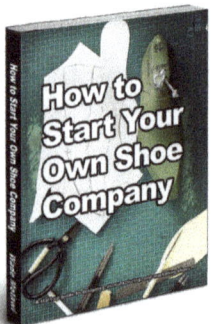

#5 *How to Start Your Own Shoe Company*
Build your brand, your business, and your dreams.
Written for everyone who dreams of starting their own shoe company. You will identify with the brand building challenges and uncover the solutions to the crucial steps such as creating your brand identity, legally setting up your company, registering your trademarks and patents, getting your shoes designed, built, paid for, and finally, marketing and selling your shoes.

SHOEMAKERS ACADEMY

Online Shoemaking Courses
Shoemaking for Designers and Brand Builders
How to Select Shoe Materials
Sneaker Authentication Basics
Creating Footwear Specifications
Footwear Cost Calculation
Footwear Cost Engineering
Footwear Inspection and Quality Control
Building a Modern Shoe Factory
Footwear Sustainability Strategies
Footwear Fitting & Comfort
Footwear Import Duty

Text Books Available Now:
How Shoes are Made
Footwear Pattern Making and Last Design
Shoe Material Design Guide
How to Start Your Own Shoe Company
How to Spot Fake Sneakers
Cómo se hacen los zapatos
Cómo empezar tu propia empresa de calzado
Guía para el diseño de materiales de calzado
Patronaje de calzado y diseño de hormas
鞋子是怎样制成的

Coming Soon:
Starting Your Shoe Business
Shoe Types and Constructions
How to Design Shoes
DIY Shoemaking for Beginners
The Footwear Process Development to Production
Footwear Development Factory Communications
Footwear Marketing & Merchandising

www.ingramcontent.com/pod-product-compliance
Lightning Source LLC
Chambersburg PA
CBHW042356030426
42336CB00030B/3495

9781735883335